The MINUTE taker's

HANDBOOK

Lee Comer
Paul Ticher

DIRECTORY OF SOCIAL CHANGE

Published by
The Directory of Social Change
24 Stephenson Way
London NW1 2DP
Tel: 020 7209 5151, fax: 020 7391 4804
e-mail: books@dsc.org.uk
from whom further copies and a full publications list are available.

The Directory of Social Change is a Registered Charity no. 800517

First published 2002

ISBN 1 900360 99 3

British Library Cataloguing in Publication Data
A catalogue record for this book is available from the British Library

Text and cover designed by Sarah Nicholson

Typeset, printed and bound by Stephen Austin, Hertford

Other Directory of Social Change departments in London:
Courses and conferences tel: 020 7209 4949
Charityfair/Charity Centre tel: 020 7209 1015
Publicity tel: 020 7391 4900
Research tel: 020 7391 4880

Directory of Social Change Northern Office:
Federation House, Hope Street, Liverpool L1 9BW
Courses and conferences tel: 0151 708 0117
Research tel: 0151 708 0136

Contents

PART THREE
During the meeting

PART FOUR
After the meeting

PART FIVE
Questions and specific situations

About the series

Series editor: Alison Baxter

This series of starter guides is aimed primarily at those who are new to the voluntary sector. The series is designed for people involved with charities or voluntary organisations or community groups of any size. All the titles offer practical, straightforward advice to enable readers to get the most out of their roles and responsibilities.

Also available in this series:
The Charity Treasurer's Handbook
Gareth G. Morgan
2002
The Charity Trustee's Handbook
Mike Eastwood
2001

Other guides planned for 2002 will cover areas such as charitable status and fundraising.

For further information, please contact the Directory of Social Change (see page 167 for details).

Foreword

Many hundreds of people have attended the authors' Minute Taking Skills courses over the last ten years. Each participant had a story to tell. For some, minute taking was a troublesome chore, for others it was a major cause of anxiety. Working in the voluntary sector should offer job satisfaction and a sense of doing something worthwhile, but this is a distant dream for the majority of minute takers, who wrestle tirelessly to tranform their notes of chaotic meetings into intelligible minutes. When hardly anyone bothers to read them, the injustice is keenly felt.

Many of the participants' experiences and suggestions have been incorporated into this book. It has been written for them, and for all minute takers in the voluntary sector. We hope that they will use this book to influence those who attend meetings and those who chair them, to recognise the importance of the minute-taker's role. When meetings are managed properly, the minute taker might even go home at the end of the day with a share in the sense of achievement of a worthwhile job being done well.

Acknowledgements

The authors would like to thank Richard Peters and Gill Taylor for their support and forbearance in the preparation of this book. We are indebted to Sandy Adirondack and James Sinclair Taylor for their work on *The Voluntary Sector Legal Handbook*, without which several chapters of this book would have been much harder to write.

About the authors

Lee Comer

Lee worked as a secretary before training as a teacher. She has been active for over 30 years in a wide variety of voluntary, arts and not-for-profit organisations and has held management positions in local government, youth work and in the arts. In 1991 she helped to run a training programme for arts practitioners and has been a full-time freelance trainer ever since. She is a regular trainer for the Directory of Social Change, Councils for Voluntary Service and other voluntary sector organisations. In addition to her minute-taking course, Lee also runs fundraising and staff management courses. She lives in the Pennines in West Yorkshire.

Paul Ticher

Paul first took minutes as secretary of a student union finance committee in 1972, and since then has taken minutes for a wide range of meetings, from a local playgroup run by parents to all-day multi-agency liaison and planning meetings. He has also fulfilled most of the other committee roles at one time or another, including being treasurer of a national voluntary organisation and chair of his local school governing body.

Paul's whole career has been in the voluntary sector, and he has spent the past 11 years as an independent consultant and trainer. His focus of interest is in information management, including such areas as the use of information technology, data protection and the management of information services. Paul's other DSC publications include *Information Management for Voluntary and Community Organisations* (with Mike Powell) and *Data Protection for Voluntary Organisations*. He has also published numerous articles and research reports into aspects of IT management in the voluntary sector.

Introduction

The minute has a long and honourable history. Modern-day committees, chairs and minute secretaries could learn a great deal from the simple origin of the minute – they might seriously consider reinstating traditional methods of minute taking.

Many hundreds of years ago, when meetings first needed to be recorded in writing for parish council records, a minute of time was set aside at the end of each agenda item so that the record could be written. The chairperson summarised whatever had been discussed and agreed, and then said 'Write this down in a minute (that is, 60 seconds)'. At the end of the meeting, the minute secretary would read these minutes back to the group, and, when agreed by all present, the record would be signed as true. (Hence the phrase, still in use today, 'the minutes were taken as read'.)

When the minutes are written directly by hand into a minute book, no note taking is required. All that is required is that the meeting is well chaired, that each item is summarised by the chair, and that the text of the minute is agreed immediately before it is written. Many small voluntary organisations – and especially those without paid staff, word processors and offices – continue with this traditional approach. It has to be said that such minutes, written directly and once only by hand into a hard-bound, stitched book are very much more authentic and reliable than minutes which have been rewritten and typed several times, before finally being approved and filed some weeks or even months later.

We realise that organisations with technology, in-trays, administrative staff and lots of projects and activities to manage have become accustomed to receiving typed minutes. To some extent they are relied on, to remind staff of their tasks and responsibilities, and as a source of information and means of communication. We therefore start from the position that many organisations would find it impossible to return to the old ways of writing minutes. However, undue reliance on minutes – and the expectation that the minute taker can realistically produce a document that fulfils these multiple purposes – can become a time-consuming burden and a wasteful exercise which serves little, if any, useful purpose.

We also recognise that there are many different types of meeting. We have taken the management committee or board as our 'typical' example; these meetings have formal requirements and ways of working that must be in any professional minute-taker's repertoire. However, the principles apply to any meeting. We have included suggestions at appropriate points for how a variety of situations might be handled, from small team meetings to wider consultations and forums.

This book aims to help you to avoid the pitfalls and to produce the most useful minutes possible, with the least effort. The book has three main themes. It looks at what should (and should not) be included in your minutes, how they should be laid out and how to achieve that aim.

The fundamental role of minutes is to provide a legally sound record of decisions and of the work of a committee or group. Anything else is almost always a distortion of their purpose. The key points are that:
- Minutes must show that a meeting which took decisions did so in a legally valid way.
- Minutes must record the decisions accurately and dispassionately.
- Where decisions set a precedent, or where the meeting has to be accountable to a wider group, the minutes may need to record the reasons for a decision.
- Minutes show that a committee or group has been carrying out its work properly, and that an organisation is holding meetings in compliance with its governing document.
- Minutes must be agreed by the meeting (or by the next meeting of the same committee or group).

Minutes are therefore intricately bound up with the work of a meeting; they are not something to be tacked on afterwards. This means that the minute taker must operate as a full member of the team running the meeting. Although many minute takers are relatively junior members of staff, this does not reflect the importance of their role. Throughout the book we show how the interaction between a good chair and a good minute taker makes the task of both much easier, and contributes in the end to the highest quality minutes.

Although the book is aimed specifically at voluntary organisations, the principles are the same for the meetings of many other organisations. We hope that clerks to school governing bodies, and those involved in church groups, political organisations and other community groups will find the book equally useful.

The first section of the book looks more closely at what minutes are for and the role of the minute taker. We then look at the minute-taker's tasks before, during and after the meeting.

One thing we stress is that preparation before the meeting will greatly reduce the amount of work after the meeting. We suggest simple ways to ensure that as a minute taker you can go into every meeting with all the equipment, background knowledge and information you need to carry out your job competently and efficiently.

During the meeting, many people worry their note-taking skills will let them down, and that they will either write too much or miss important points. While the conduct of the chair can do a lot to make the task easier, minute takers cannot usually choose their chairs, and may have very little influence over them. We therefore look at how to cope effectively, even in imperfect circumstances.

After the meeting, the main questions are how to lay minutes out, what to include, and how to phrase things correctly. We believe that if minutes are used for their true purpose they should not be lengthy or detailed. Nevertheless, the task of transcribing notes from a meeting into good quality minutes is not trivial. Many people find that it can take as much time as the meeting itself. We believe that by following the suggestions in this book you will be able to reduce this time significantly.

Minute taking may not become exactly a pleasure (the title 'The Joy of Minute Taking' would perhaps not be appropriate), but it can for most people become a considerably smaller burden.

Legal considerations

A set of minutes is a legal document. We have mentioned legal issues at appropriate places in the book. We have also taken into account guidance from the Charity Commission which, while not necessarily legally binding, is generally regarded as required reading. This book does not, however, set out to give a full statement of the law. You should take qualified legal advice if you are concerned on specific points.

A note on terminology

Because minutes have a long history, going right back to when scribes used Latin, we have had to use − or at least refer to − a large number of technical terms. Although in many cases there are 'plain English' equivalents, a good minute taker must at least be familiar with these terms in case their use is appropriate, or in case other people use them during a meeting.

We have therefore included a glossary at the end of the book where many formal and technical terms are defined. If you come across an unfamiliar word, you may well find it in the glossary.

PART ONE

Minutes and the minute taker: their roles and purposes

1 Why do we take minutes?

The minutes of an organisation are among its most important documents. (In a crisis, such as flood or fire, someone should have responsibility for ensuring that, after the people are safely out of the building, rescuing the minute files is one of the next priorities.) They are a record of decisions, and proof that the organisation is conducting its business legally and properly.

One reason why taking minutes is sometimes more complicated than it might be is because minutes can have three purposes:

- as an agreed record of the decisions made by a meeting;
- as a reminder of action that people have agreed to take, or a means of following up to see whether the action has been taken;
- as a source of information for people who weren't at the meeting.

Just because minutes can have these three purposes doesn't mean you should always use them for all three. A separate report may be a better way of providing information. An action sheet may be more useful for reminding people what they have agreed to do. The minute taker does, however, have to be aware of what is expected from a particular set of minutes in order to decide what to put in and what to leave out.

The most important thing is that minutes are an *agreed record of decisions*. They have a legal status as documentary proof that decisions were made, and made in the right way. (See *Minutes must be signed*, page 91.)

Minutes may also be part of the way an organisation is *accountable* – to its clients, its members, its funders, its staff or any other 'stakeholders'. In some cases it is particularly important not just to record the decisions that were made, but also to show the process by which they were made and, in brief, why they were made. For example, if the staff ask for a ten per cent pay increase, it may be important to record why the organisation has decided only to offer five per cent. If a committee decides to close one of the projects run by an organisation, its minutes may have to show that it took account of the views of all those affected before reaching its decision.

Don't get distracted by the fact that minutes can have any number of secondary uses. For example, minutes form an important part of the history of an organisation – which is especially fascinating if the organisation has been in existence for hundreds of years, such as some missionary societies or city livery companies. This is an argument for producing good quality minutes that will stand the test of time, but not for writing deliberately with an eye on impressing posterity.

Another secondary use of minutes is to treat them as a poor substitute for a proper information system. If people are expected to find out important information by reading minutes (or, worse, if important information is hidden in minutes in the hope that people won't read them) the minutes are not being used appropriately. When minutes are used as a source of information, it must be information that is genuinely relevant to the workings of the committee or group whose meetings they record.

Minutes should not be regarded as a primary way of communicating with people. The essence of communication is its immediacy. Communication takes place in many ways – face to face, by telephone, e-mail, fax, memo, letter, post-it note, notice board or newsletter (and doubtless through countless other means). All of these methods have inherent immediacy. Communication is also normally personalised, that is it is addressed to an individual or to a particular group. When people communicate in this way, they use direct language, active verbs and the full range of adjectives. These methods engage attention and often get the desired result.

How many people show any eagerness to read minutes of meetings that may have taken place more than a week ago? (This is often the minimum amount of time taken to issue minutes of meetings.) The minutes are already history. We know – if only subconsciously – that the minutes are for the record, and thus for reference only. Readers glance through the minutes to establish what was decided, what's coming up, what actions they are supposed to take and the date of the next meeting.

If a particular individual who wasn't at the meeting wanted to know what had happened, their first port of call would be to contact someone who was at the meeting. The last resort is to read the minutes. And if the minutes are correctly written, they will not be very informative! There might have been a heated argument. People might have lost their tempers and behaved badly. The minutes should merely note 'A full (or lengthy) discussion took place'.

❝ Can anyone ask to see our minutes? Are they a public document? **❞**

The general rule is that the only people who are entitled to see minutes are those who are entitled to attend the meeting – in other words, normally, the members of that meeting. So, for a general meeting, all the members of the association can see the minutes; for a board meeting, the members of the board, and so on.

If your organisation is a company limited by guarantee, it is subject to company law. Under this, members of the company (who may not always be the same as members of the organisation) are entitled to see the minutes of general meetings, including the annual general meeting (AGM). If they want a copy they may be charged up to 10p per 100 words (as at 1 April 2001).

The Charity Commission recommends that charities make the minutes of the AGM available to the public on request, and suggests that they may charge a reasonable fee to cover the cost of providing them.

Minutes of other meetings, including those of trustees or the management committee, do not have to be made available to the public, unless the law or your governing document says so. The minutes of school governing bodies, for example, must by law be available to the public.

You may have to provide copies of specific minutes to prove specific things. For example, banks often ask for proof, via a copy of the relevant minutes, that the opening of a new account has been properly authorised.

If it takes decisions, it needs minutes

Much of this book is, inevitably, concerned with formal meetings – of management committees, boards, trustees and the like, or their official sub-committees. But these are not the only meetings that play an important part in the running of many voluntary organisations.

Any group that takes binding decisions must record what those decisions were and how they were taken. A conference planning group must ensure that it identifies all the necessary tasks and gets them done in time. A liaison committee that agrees an order of priorities for the use of council funds must be able to show that its recommendations were arrived at in a fair way. Even a staff team deciding on a washing-up rota may be asked to prove that it was non-discriminatory.

In all these cases, the minutes must be available for the record, just in case there is ever a question about what was done and whether it was properly authorised. They may also be important tools for reminding people of the action they were supposed to take and checking that it has been done.

This does not mean that the minutes of meetings such as these will look the same, or contain the same kind of information, as those of a formal board or management committee meeting. However, the same amount of thought should go into how the minutes are written.

66 The meeting I minute is not a committee. It's an advisory group (it used to be called a steering group). Does it have to have formal signed minutes? 99

Advisory groups have certain powers, which should be set out in terms of reference. They can usually make recommendations that are referred to other committees or groups. They will probably have a quorum. Members of the advisory group may also have to prove that they attended the group's meeting. Advisory groups should therefore be treated in the same way as committees. Signed minutes and signing in to prove attendance are both necessary.

2 The minute taker is part of a team

The minute taker is an important person. The minute taker and the chair, and possibly others, jointly share responsibility for the conduct, management and record keeping of the meeting. There are several distinct roles in a meeting. Some of these may be combined in one person, but they need not always be; it is worth knowing what the different roles are, and working out who fills them in the meetings you minute.

Chair

The chair runs the meeting and makes sure that everything happens properly, giving people a fair chance to speak, ensuring that people focus on the issues and keep to the agenda, and ensuring that clear decisions are made. The chair should be familiar with the agenda items and should be able to anticipate how the meeting will proceed. From the minute-taker's point of view, it is important that the chair summarises every decision, not just so that the minute taker is clear what the outcome is, but also so that all the members – who each have a share of the responsibility for the actions of the committee or group – know what has been decided.

The chair of an organisation is not always the person who chairs the meetings. Often the governing document will set out rules for this, but in other cases, or when the chair is not available, it may be up to the meeting to choose its own chair.

The chair of the meeting may also be involved in drawing up the agenda, especially if they are also chair of the organisation, with wider responsibilities. However, it is quite possible for the committee secretary (see below) to take on the task of preparing the agenda.

It is normally unwise for the chair and minute-taking roles to be combined, since the chair has to be alert to all the personal interaction taking place, while the minute taker has to be listening carefully to the sense of the discussion. However, if the old way of minuting is adopted – where the minute is written and read out immediately after the discussion – there is no reason why the chair shouldn't also write the minutes.

Secretary

The title 'secretary' has so many different possible meanings that it is not much used in relation to meetings. However, there is a clear role for someone who guides the business of the meeting and assists the committee or group in carrying out its decisions. We have called this role 'secretary' in this book.

The secretary will do all or most of the preparation for the meeting and much of the follow-up. This might include:

- drawing up the agenda (possibly in conjunction with the chair);
- inviting people to attend and speak;
- ensuring that anyone who is required to be there (for example to report on their area of work) is available;
- asking the relevant people to write briefing papers and reports before the meeting;
- sending out papers in advance of the meeting;
- giving advice to the chair about the business, both before and during the meeting;
- reporting back to the meeting about actions decided on at the last meeting;
- writing letters, researching information or arranging further meetings in response to decisions of the meeting;
- making arrangements for equipment (flip charts or projectors) and refreshments during the meeting;
- arranging to pay travel expenses to participants.

In many organisations the chief officer plays the role of secretary for the meetings of the main management committee or board and for the more important sub-committees such as personnel and finance. The secretary may also take the minutes, but this is a task that is often delegated – along with jobs like arranging the room for the meeting and organising the refreshments.

Clerk

The clerk's role is concerned not with the business of the meeting, but with the process. The clerk may have to:

- keep the membership records for the committee or group, and alert people when their terms of office expire;
- make sure that members declare any interests (see *Glossary*, page 160) that might affect (or appear to affect) their decisions;

- induct new members onto a committee or into a group;
- notify Companies House and the Charity Commission of changes to the membership of a board or management committee;
- ensure that the calling notice for a meeting goes out in good time, to the right people, and contains the right information including the agenda;
- advise the meeting on its procedures and legal responsibilities, and what to do when unusual events occur;
- chair the meeting while it is electing a chair.

Some of these duties may be undertaken by the company secretary or chief officer, and some may be combined with the minute-taker's role. In less formal meetings any of these tasks, except the last one, may be undertaken by the chair.

Minute taker

So where does all this leave the minute taker? Depending on what other roles they play, the minute taker may be involved in many of the tasks that surround an effective meeting. The tasks that belong specifically to the minute taker include:

- supervising signing-in procedures, attendance sheets and the quorum;
- receiving and reporting apologies – although this could be part of the clerk's duties, it usually falls to the minute taker;
- ensuring that papers for discussion and past minutes for reference are available during the meeting;
- writing minutes during the meeting, or taking notes and producing draft minutes after the meeting;
- alerting the chair to any gaps in procedure during the meeting which will show up in the minutes – failure to make clear decisions, deviation from the agenda, lack of a quorum, for example;
- ensuring that approved minutes are signed and filed properly.

Duties which do not sit well with the minute-taker's responsibilities include:

- meeting and greeting guests and visitors – because you need to be preparing for your role in the meeting and ensuring that everyone has the papers they need;
- making tea and coffee or serving refreshments that arrive during the meeting – because it takes the minute taker away from the meeting.

Working as a team

It is unusual for there to be four people involved in managing a meeting – chair, secretary, clerk and minute taker – but there are often three people who combine these roles.

Everything goes much more smoothly if these people work as a team, understanding and respecting each other's roles, and liaising closely to make sure there are no gaps between them. It is particularly important that the minute taker and the chair have a good understanding. (See *A protocol between the minute taker and chair*, page 13.)

Wherever possible, the minute taker and chair should meet together before the meeting begins to go over the agenda and to agree the details of how they will manage and record the meeting. We recognise that this is not always possible. Some chairs just will not accept the importance of such liaison. Others are not available, for reasons of time, because they come from a distance, or because the meetings are not always chaired by the same person.

In these circumstances, it may be helpful for the minute taker to liaise instead with other members of the team, such as the secretary. They may be able to provide much of the information that the chair would otherwise have about the content and conduct of the meeting. They may also be able to intercede with the chair and suggest the minute-taker's role be taken more seriously.

As keeper of the records, the minute taker should advise the chair about outstanding matters that need to be carried over to future meetings. With this in mind, we recommend that it is best practice for the minute taker also to be involved at the planning stage of every meeting. This should help to prevent the all-too-common problem of being called in to minute a meeting without knowing anything about the agenda items to be discussed.

❝Is it possible to take minutes and participate in the meeting at the same time? **❞**

Yes, provided that:

- the minute taker is familiar with the subject matter;
- the minutes are limited to decisions and action points;
- sufficient time is allowed for the minute taker to record the decisions and action points at the end of each agenda item (usually one minute of time is sufficient to write 30 words).

The minute taker should sit next to the chair

The importance of the minute-taker's role at a meeting is at odds with the practice, common in many voluntary organisations, of placing the minute taker as far away as possible from the action. It is not unheard of for the minute taker to be seated unobtrusively in the corner or, worse, away from the table altogether. Apart from being rude, this fails to recognise the importance of their role in helping the meeting to run properly.

The minute taker should sit next to the chair so that:

- he or she can play a full role in helping to manage the meeting;
- the chair can sign the minutes easily when they have been approved;
- the minute taker can write any corrections by hand into the file copy of the minutes, under the chair's supervision;
- either of them can alert the other, discreetly, to particular problems;
- the chair can refer to papers or previous reports which the minute taker has brought to the meeting;
- the minute taker can help the chair to monitor time keeping.

Informal and unstructured meetings

Even in an informal meeting, most of the roles discussed above still have to be carried out, but perhaps not in such a rigidly defined way. Someone still has to make sure that the meeting runs properly. Someone still has to take responsibility for the business. Someone has to be concerned with the process. And someone has to record the decisions and show that they were properly made.

For informal meetings that are within an organisation – team meetings or working groups, for example – it may be relatively easy to see who has these different roles, or there may be a manager who decides. Looser structures may give rise to problems. In a forum it may not be obvious who has to follow up the decisions. Liaison groups may elect a different chair each time, making it hard for them to prepare or build up a relationship with the other members of the team.

If you are asked to take the minutes for an informal or unstructured meeting, it is always worth trying to find out who fulfils the other key roles, in order to at least establish contact with them and explore their expectations of your role and how the team will work.

Natural breaks

No one can work effectively for hours on end without a break, but those who plan meetings don't always take this into account. In order to 'save time' participants may be able to leave the meeting to fetch drinks and refreshments while the meeting carries on. A sandwich lunch may even be served without allowing the meeting to break.

Even when a person's time is precious, they are not exempt from normal human needs, and a meeting in which people are tired, hungry, stiff or needing the toilet is unlikely to make good decisions. The number of emergencies so serious that people genuinely need to be put under such pressure is small. If the meeting is failing to make its decisions in the time allotted, the likelihood is that it has either been badly planned or is being badly chaired.

For the minute taker, a meeting without breaks is even worse. The minute taker cannot opt out of particular items or afford to lose concentration, and would find it difficult to eat and take notes at the same time. No one should be expected to cope with such a situation.

Although people's peak attention span lasts about 25 minutes, it is probably realistic to allow uninterrupted sessions of up to an hour and half. This might be stretched to two hours if the meeting is certain to finish by then. Any meeting that is longer must have a break of at least ten minutes in every hour and a half when everyone, including the minute taker, can go to the toilet, stretch their legs and preferably get refreshments. This must be a genuine break; if the minute taker is expected to make the tea and coffee or sort out participants' travel claims, they are not getting a break.

Because of the degree of concentration required of the minute taker, it is also reasonable to share the duties during meetings that are particularly large and complex or that last all day or longer. The two minute takers could either both sit in, swapping over between items, or could take half a day at a time each.

Exercise

Think about the meetings you minute. Who fulfils the following roles:

- chair
- secretary
- clerk?

Is everyone clear about who does what? Do any of the tasks get neglected because no one sees them as their responsibility?

A protocol between the minute taker and chair

The chair and the minute taker in far too many meetings have a grossly unequal status. This can make it hard for the minute taker to be assertive in carrying out their role. When the minute-taker's role is not properly understood, the chair may fail to give them the opportunity to make their full contribution. It may therefore be worth having an agreement, or protocol, setting out how the chair and minute taker will work together. This does not have to be formal, if the relationship is good; the most important thing is that both parties should feel happy with what is going on.

The protocol between the chair and the minute taker should include the following points:

1 The chair summarises at the end of each agenda item.

2 The minute taker can ask for clarification if an issue, decision or point is not clear.

3 The minute taker can ask the meeting 'How would you like that minuted?'.

4 It is the chair's role, rather than the minute-taker's, to decide whether something should, or should not be minuted (to cover those times where participants may try to insist that a comment should, or should not, be minuted).

5 The chair will give the minute taker clear guidance if an item needs to be minuted separately as a confidential minute (see *When and how to write a confidential minute*, page 135).

6 The minute taker has the right, during the meeting, to draw the chair's attention to any problem or omission, and vice versa.

7 The proper procedure regarding tabled papers and any other business is followed (see *'Tabled' papers*, page 35).

8   The minute taker will monitor the quorum and alert the chair if numbers fall too low.

9   The minute taker and chair should agree on which of them will have the main responsibility for monitoring whether the meeting is keeping to time.

10 The meeting will be allowed natural breaks at reasonable intervals.

PART **TWO**

Before the meeting

3 The importance of preparation

It is far from unheard of for someone to be quietly working at their desk when a senior colleague comes over and says 'We're about to start a meeting, and our minute taker has called in sick. Would you do it?'.

Now the correct answer to this question is really 'No, I'm sorry, I won't', for reasons that will become apparent. In reality, of course, you have no choice and have to make the best of a bad job. It would be worthwhile in such a situation, however, to bargain for as much preparation time as you can, even if it delays the start of the meeting slightly.

Preparation before the meeting is essential for good minute taking. There are three main reasons:

- to reduce the amount of work you have to do during the meeting, so that you have more time to concentrate on what is happening;
- to ensure that you understand what is happening in the meeting, so that the notes you take record the information you will need when you come to write up the minutes (no more and no less);
- to establish a relationship with the chair and other key people, leading to good team work during the meeting.

The kind of preparation you need to do will vary, depending on whether the meeting is one of a cycle that you regularly minute, or one that you are new to, but the main elements are the same:

- Become familiar with the issues and background.
- Make sure you can identify who is 'present' and who is 'in attendance'.
- Understand the agenda.
- Establish your protocol with the chair (see previous chapter).
- Prepare all the papers you will need for the meeting.
- Assemble the equipment you will need.
- Be aware of the meeting's governing document and procedures.

This preparation takes time – time that is well spent.

We would also recommend that the minute taker and chair arrive at the venue at least 15 minutes before the meeting is due to start, so that they can discuss how they will work together. They can then also ensure that the seating arrangements allow them to sit next to each other, with adequate table space for their papers and notes.

If it is not possible to meet the chair, the minute taker should still be able to prepare before the meeting. At the very least, you should familiarise yourself with the agenda, read the accompanying reports, highlighting any particular points, and read through previous minutes of these meetings.

Understand what is being discussed

Few meetings take place in isolation. If there is a special, one-off meeting, it is quite likely that the person arranging it will have to write something down explaining to everyone what the meeting is about. You may well find that this, plus your pre-meeting briefing with the chair, is enough to give you all the information you need.

Most meetings, however, have a history behind them. Many of the participants will know what has been discussed before. They may want to continue old arguments, or chase up things that should have happened in the past. When this happens, they will often launch straight in, without going over the background for your benefit (or for anyone else who isn't as experienced as they are).

When people are making decisions they often have to take into account financial considerations or statistics. 'The salary for this post is £18,345, plus London weighting. With direct on-costs that comes to £24,287. Let's call it £25,000 for the budget to be on the safe side.' 'We saw 274 clients at the drop-in centre last month. This week we've had 80 already. At this rate the total number will be 20% up on last year.' Your final minute will not necessarily need to include all – or any – of the actual figures, if they are not an essential part of the decision. But you usually need to have a sense of what is going on so that you can assess what is relevant.

People who are on familiar territory also tend to use a lot of jargon without explaining what it means. They use abbreviations, acronyms and shorthand ways of referring to other people and organisations. When people in a meeting talk about 'The Centre' they may mean 'The TAD Centre', which refers to 'The Training and Development Centre', which in fact is a business development and conference centre. Unless you know this, any decision to arrange accommodation for a visiting trainer at 'The Centre' is likely to leave you mystified, and unable to record an accurate minute. You could easily confuse it with 'The Project' where the training course has been booked to take place.

All this means that part of your preparation for the meeting should be aimed at ensuring you don't get tripped up any more often than absolutely necessary. You should consider:

- Studying the agenda, if you have not already been part of drawing it up.
- Reading past minutes and background papers to pick up jargon, abbreviations and common themes or recurrent issues. In particular you should notice any 'unfinished business' that is likely to come back (whether it is on this agenda or not).
- Reading through any background papers being sent out for this meeting.
- Talking to key people who may be presenting items for discussion or decision. You may find that the treasurer, for example, can tell you enough about the likely outcome of the budget discussion to enable you (and the treasurer, if they are amenable) to write down in rough terms the only three possible outcomes beforehand, leaving a few gaps for any figures that still need to be agreed.
- Asking colleagues to explain any abbreviations or jargon you are unfamiliar with.

As part of your preparation, it may also be worth checking that other people have prepared their contributions properly. Do background papers clearly relate to specific agenda items? If an item is down for decision, is there a clear recommendation or set of options? Is there a summary so that people do not have to flick through a long document during the meeting? If an item contains complicated facts and figures does the accompanying paper explain which ones are most important, and why? (It is said that only one person in twenty really understands numerical information. People who work with numbers all the time tend to forget this, and assume that participants will be able to draw their own conclusions from a sheet of figures.)

Know who the people are

The minutes of a meeting do not have to record each person's individual comments. In fact, it is very bad practice to do so (see *Minutes are not a verbatim record*, page 105). So – courtesy apart – why do you need to know who the people are in a meeting?

One reason is to check that the signing-in procedures, attendance record and apologies for absence are accurate (see *All meetings need an attendance record*, page 80). People who sign in are likely to treat it as a chore; their signatures won't necessarily be very legible. It is quite likely that the members of the meeting will know each other well, and someone might well say 'Roger asked me to give his apologies; he's had to go to the Nottingham office'. If you can't decipher the signatures and don't know who 'Roger' is, you will have to do more work afterwards to find out before you can type up the attendance record.

If someone leaves during the meeting you *must* record the time and the point on the agenda where they left. You can't do this if you don't know who they are; better to have the information than to interrupt the meeting to find out.

If you are monitoring the quorum, or if any decision comes to a vote, you will need to know which of the people present are entitled to vote. Although the chair may check this, those present may not. In the proposed protocol (see previous chapter) we suggest that the minute taker should have this responsibility.

Another reason for knowing who people are is to help you assess each person's contribution to a topic. The treasurer will not necessarily say 'Speaking as the Treasurer ...', but if they go on to make a point about the financial viability of a proposal, their views are likely to carry weight and may well contribute to the reasoning behind the eventual decision.

Where people are presenting an item, it is worth knowing who they are, so that you can draw them into your preparations, or follow them up afterwards. If someone talks about a field trip to Hungary, you might find it very useful to get a list from them of how to spell the names of the places they visited. If a report is likely to include lots of facts and figures, you may want to talk to the relevant person in advance, so that you can follow the discussion better during the meeting.

Occasionally it will be necessary to know exactly who a person is. They may ask for a specific reservation about a decision to be minuted. If the chair agrees to their request, that is one of the few times when a contribution would be related to a named person, as shown here:

Decision: It was agreed that the 'no alcohol' rule would be relaxed for the summer fête. The committee noted William Brown's strong disagreement with this, on the grounds that it would set an unwelcome precedent.

Research before the meeting

You need to think about who is coming to the meeting beforehand, and then how to identify them during the meeting.

Before the meeting you should, if possible, get a list of who is expected to attend. Your sources of information might include:

- the membership list and/or attendance record from past meetings;
- the minutes of past meetings, for those who attended and those who apologised;
- the agenda, which might show that someone is coming for a particular item;
- the distribution list for papers and agendas;
- if necessary, the record of elections or appointments to the committee or working group, which may be in its minutes, but may be in the minutes of a parent body (such as AGM minutes in the case of a management committee or board, main committee minutes in the case of a sub-committee or working group).

Formal committee meetings will normally have a list of named members. This list should be readily available, but you do need to be aware that the distribution list for agendas and papers may not be the same as the voting membership (see *How to tell if a meeting is valid*, page 46). So that you can record the minutes accurately, you have to know about both the actual members, and anyone else likely to attend (and the reason why they are coming).

Where a meeting is less formal or less structured, it may not be possible to identify people in advance. The parents' association at school is open to any parent; apart from a few regulars you may find different people coming each time. A discussion forum may involve representatives from organisations who just turn up for the meetings that interest them, and so on. There may be fewer reasons to know who people are, but it is no less important if your minutes are to be accurate. In these cases you need to use some of the techniques described below.

Techniques during the meeting

You may not be the only one in the room who is keen to know who everyone is. It is rare to find a meeting without at least one new person, and in some cases most people will not know each other. A good chair will always make introductions, or ask people to introduce themselves, at the start of the meeting – good for the minute taker and good for everyone else.

When you know in advance who should be attending the meeting, two options particularly worth considering are:

- A plan of where people are sitting. Draw a rough plan of the table beforehand. When people arrive whom you already know, put their names in the appropriate places. As you discover who the others are (during the introductions, perhaps), slot them in. If you have a list of names already, you only need write down the initials. Remember to update the plan if people arrive late or leave early.

- Name plates in front of each person. This is particularly useful where the other participants may not know each other well. Make up the name plates beforehand. Use A4 card, folded lengthways, and write the names in large, clear letters. Make sure you put the name on both sides, so that people can tell who they are sitting next to as well as who is opposite. Ask people to take their name card as they come in, or as the meeting starts.

When you do not have a list of participants in advance, you will probably have to rely on making a seating plan as the meeting progresses. The information for this may come from:

- The signing-in sheet. If people add their names in order as the paper goes round the table, this may give you what you need, but it does depend on people writing clearly.

- Introductions at the start of the meeting. But if people mumble, or arrive late, you may miss some of the names, and you have to write fast to get full names down.

- If you don't catch a name, can't decipher it, or if it is unfamiliar to you, you may have to ask during the meeting for people to say again who they are, or catch them privately afterwards or in the break.

- At worst, if you miss a name completely, note down any key identification, being careful to keep it neutral ('woman in pink cardigan', for example, is fine, but 'loud-mouth' is not) and ask a colleague afterwards to help you identify them.

Two options which are sometimes tried, but which tend to work less well are:

1 People announcing who they are when they speak. Unless you have a very determined chair, the first few people may do this, but then people get caught up in the discussion and forget.

2 Name badges. People are often reluctant to wear these, or put them on their jacket when they arrive then take the jacket off, or write the name so small that you can't read it from the other side of the table.

4 A good meeting needs a good agenda

The agenda identifies the matters to be discussed at a meeting. A formal meeting must have an agenda that is circulated before the meeting to everyone who is expected to attend. (See *How to tell if a meeting is valid*, page 46.) Even the most informal of meetings will benefit from an agenda. (The word originally meant 'the things that are to be done'.) The agenda:

- tells people in advance what will be discussed, so that they can prepare;
- reminds people during the meeting, so that nothing gets left out;
- helps the chair to manage the timing of the meeting;
- helps the minute taker to structure their notes during the meeting and write up the minutes afterwards.

The agenda must be headed by the following information (see example below):

- name of the organisation
- name of the particular meeting or group
- date, time and venue of the meeting.

Newtown Community Centre, Old Rd, Newtown, Leics.

Fundraising and Publicity Sub-Committee Meeting

Date of Meeting :   Monday 9 March 2001 at 7.30pm – 9.30pm
Place: Newtown Community Centre Meeting Room

Agenda

Some minute takers will share responsibility with the chair and secretary for planning and managing the meeting, and for typing and circulating the agenda. This is a good opportunity both to ensure that the agenda is well written and also to carry out some of the minute-taker's necessary preparation for the meeting. Although it is not strictly a minute-taking role to prepare the agenda, a good agenda is related to a good meeting and subsequently to good minutes, so we include a discussion here.

The dangers of a poor agenda

Some voluntary organisations have a rather lazy approach to planning their meetings. The person preparing the agenda may receive items verbally or on scraps of paper at the last minute. Worse, topics may be suggested at the start of the meeting or, worse still, brought up under any other business. This may be common practice for small, informal working groups but it is not acceptable for meetings at which decisions are to be taken.

Unfortunately, old habits die hard. Last minute cobbling together of an uninformative agenda does little for the participants, and even less for the minute taker. Agendas that are thrown together often look like this:

Apologies
Minutes of previous meeting
Matters arising
Correspondence received
Finance report
Manager's report

      1) Premises
      2) Local government re-organisation

Any other business
Date and time of next meeting

Participants – and the minute taker – will come to the meeting with little idea of what these agenda items are about. The secretary or the chair may have the knowledge, but people will have to wait until the meeting takes place to become any wiser. In addition, there is no indication in this agenda of the relative importance of the various items. Some may be trivial, others urgent and important. Meetings built around agendas like these can degenerate very quickly. All too often, the participants will spend an hour discussing the first three or four, less important items and then run out of time for the later items which require thorough discussion before important decisions can be reached.

Like the hapless participants, the minute taker is unable to become familiar with the subject matter to be discussed and is therefore at a distinct disadvantage when it comes to minuting the meeting.

Agendas like the one above have long passed their sell-by date. Proper preparation of the agenda will make the meeting easier to chair, and to minute, and will ensure that participants have a clearer understanding of the various items to be discussed at the meeting.

How to write a good agenda

Best practice in preparing the agenda involves some preparatory thought and planning. Instead of listing, for example:

Health and safety

the agenda would include the subject line followed by a brief description:

Health and safety
The implications of recent minibus legislation   For discussion

Each agenda item/subject should have a brief description, a clear purpose and, ideally, an estimate of the time to be allotted to it. The person responsible for presenting the item to the meeting should also be indicated on the agenda.

The agenda we started out with could be rewritten as in the example on page 27. You will see that each item on the agenda:

- is clearly described;
- has a clear purpose (reason why it is on the agenda);
- is numbered;
- has approximate timings;
- identifies, where appropriate, the person responsible for presenting the item.

Note also that the importance of the items which are 'for decision' is reflected in the extra time allocated to them.

There are just five possible purposes for items being on an agenda. These purposes will apply to all organisations, regardless of their sphere of activity and regardless of the types of meetings they hold. These five purposes are:

Agenda item	Purpose	Person presenting	Approx. time
1. Apologies for absence	Record		2 mins
2. Minutes of previous meeting held on 5 Dec 2000	**Approval**	Chair	5 mins
3. Matters arising *excluding* those included in agenda items 6 and 7	Information	Team/Staff/ Chair	10 mins
4. Correspondence			
Information received from HQ about proposed changes to affiliation procedures	Information	Manager	5 mins
5. Finance			
5.1 Budget report Jan 01 – June 01	Information	Treasurer	10 mins
5.2 Fundraising proposals for 2002 **(Report 5.2 enclosed)**	**Decision**	Treasurer	30 mins
6. Manager's reports			
6.1 Advice Centre's work April 01–June 01	Information	Manager	10 mins
6.2 Premises **(Report 6.2 enclosed)** Proposal to convert photocopying room to an interview room, to ease pressure on client waiting times	**Decision**	Manager	20 mins
7. Local government re-organisation (Briefing paper 7 enclosed) Funding implications of proposed re-organisation of Newtown Borough Council	Discussion	Chair	15 mins
8. Any other business			
9. Date and time of next meeting	Record		

- for information only
- for discussion
- for decision
- for approval
- for the record.

Each purpose is described below.

For information only

Items are often on the agenda for information only because those attending need to be kept informed about activities and developments. They may also be there as part of the meeting's contribution to monitoring and accountability. The minutes need to show that the meeting was aware of particular information or had been informed about an event or action. The following examples would fall in this category:

- Verbal or written reports about work, activities and progress.
- Regular statistics the meeting may need in order to monitor what is happening, or just to be reassured that the person producing the statistics knows what is going on.
- General items of interest or information, such as staff changes, external events and reminders of holiday closing dates.

Those attending the meeting 'receive' the item. They may discuss or question aspects of the information but, ultimately, the purpose is to 'note' the information received. (See *Finding the right words for other situations*, page 121.)

The manager's report is a regular feature on most agendas. More often than not, these items are purely for information, as in the example below:

Manager's Report   For information (15 mins)
Verbal report on Newtown Community Centre's activities Jan–March 2001

This type of item is very difficult to minute, as it is rarely clear how much of the information to include. It is often better if the person presenting the information is asked to put it into a short written summary that can accompany the agenda or be given to the minute taker for incorporation into the typed minutes. At the same time, any parts of the report that are not simply for information but actually for discussion or decision can be separated out.

The person planning a meeting needs to be careful not to overdo items for information only. Many organisations have found, to their cost, that they can waste a great deal of time. Typically, a few people discuss items while most participants twiddle their thumbs, uninterested in the topic. (The matters being discussed could, so often, be solved by a private conversation between the two people concerned.) It has therefore become increasingly common to dispense altogether with agenda items for information only. Instead, any information items are listed as an appendix to the agenda, together with brief descriptions, and a contact name, so that participants receiving the agenda can decide for themselves whether they wish to know more about the subject. The appendix could look like the one below.

Appendix: Items for information only

Users' Open day held on 18 September 2001
A one-page users' evaluation report, on the benefits of the Open Day.
Contact: Paul Manning, Co-ordinator, for more information and a copy of the report.

Letter on health and safety review
The Council has announced a health and safety review for all organisations it funds.
Contact: Premises Manager for details and timing.

An alternative is to include information items on the agenda, so that people have the opportunity to ask questions on the topic. If there are no questions, the matter is not discussed, and the minutes need only indicate that the information was received and noted, or simply noted. (It is always better to use the term 'noted', which signifies that the committee was made fully aware of the item, rather than 'received', which could imply that the committee did not absorb the content of the item.)

For small pieces of information it may be possible to include the full information in the agenda:

Centenary appeal   For information only (1 min)
To note that the appeal has now reached £15,668, and that the next event is the summer fête

See *Finding the right words for other situations*, page 121, for more on how to write up this type of item.

If the meeting is running short of time but the information is on the agenda or attached, items which are for information only can safely be skipped over, so that enough time is left for the more important items.

For discussion

Items which are for discussion are usually more important than items which are for information. They are issues of concern to the participants at the meeting, where ideas and contributions to a debate are aired and given serious consideration. Such items may appear regularly on the agenda and may lay the ground for future decision making.

Items for discussion may include any or all of the following:

- Preliminary ideas about new policies, practices and projects.
- Responses to new developments.
- Gathering in of ideas, suggestions about existing or new areas of work.
- Ways forward on policy issues such as equal opportunities.

Here is an example:

Non-smoking Policy (Report No. 2 attached)   For discussion (20 mins)
To consider the possibility of introducing a non-smoking policy in the Community Centre. In addition, to consider the results of a survey of users' views on the possible introduction of such a policy.

For decision

Items for decision have priority over all other items and should be placed high on the agenda. They always require thorough discussion and clear decision-making procedures. It is therefore vital that agenda items which require a decision are clearly identified on all agendas, regardless of whether the meeting is formally constituted. Here is an example:

Staffing (Report No. 5 attached)   For decision (30 mins)
Proposal to appoint an additional part-time administrative assistant

For approval

Items for approval (or ratification) are included on agendas in order that decisions and actions already taken can be shown to have been properly authorised. Items for approval differ from items for decision in that the decision has already been taken elsewhere, before the meeting. In many organisations, for example, paid staff members have authority to spend money within budgets which have already been agreed, but they still need to report back and seek final approval from the relevant committee. Such items, though normally dealt with quite speedily, are very important.

Items for approval may also cover 'Chair's action' – where the chair has done something in an emergency, without time to call a meeting, but the action now needs to be ratified.

Where another meeting reports back to your meeting, you need to be careful to distinguish between a sub-committee which may have delegated powers to take decisions on behalf of the main meeting, and a working group which can only make recommendations (see *Glossary*, page 160). The minutes of a sub-committee will be received and noted (for information), while the recommendations of a working group will need to be approved.

Here are two examples:

3. Photocopier maintenance contract (copy attached, marked Appendix A)
   For approval (5 mins)
   To approve the 2001-02 maintenance contract with J. Bloggs and Co. for £350 p/a

4. Grant awards to community-based organisations
   For approval (15 mins)
   Recommendations of the Grant Panel to award grants totalling £26,000 to community-based organisations in Newtown District.
   (The full list would follow.)

For the record

Items for the record are the bits and bobs on the agenda. They appear on the agenda because they must appear in the minutes.

Here are some examples:

* apologies received (from those who could not attend the meeting);
* signing and agreeing the minutes of the previous meeting (including minuting any corrections to them);
* the name of the person who chaired the meeting;
* correspondence received;
* date of the next meeting.

Procedures for placing items on the agenda

In most organisations, items arrive on the agenda in a variety of ways. There will normally be some routine, repeated items and some current issues specific to that meeting. Often, the whole agenda will be drawn up by the secretary and/or the chair, without any wider consultation. This may be entirely practical – they never leave enough time so the agenda is prepared in a rush; it may just be an out-dated habit; or it may even be a well-guarded control mechanism.

We recommend greater transparency, ensuring that all members of a group have an opportunity to put items forward. If the chair refused to place an item on the agenda, they would, at the very least, be obliged to offer an explanation, which could be challenged. The procedures for putting items forward should be the same for all. We suggest using a standard pro-forma, such as the one shown on page 33.

This example can be customised to any organisation, and distributed to all who attend the meetings, giving everyone the same opportunity to put forward their items in time for the agenda to be typed up and circulated. The pro-forma requires people to write a brief description of their item, and to identify a purpose. It has the added advantage of deterring people from putting trivial matters on agendas.

Uses and abuses of any other business

The example agenda on page 27 includes, as item 8, any other business (AOB). This may appear as a godsend to members who are overworked or lazy. Its presence signals to them their right to raise any item of their choice at the end of the meeting. It also carries a strong suggestion that the normal procedures for placing items on the agenda in advance of the meeting can, with impunity, be bypassed.

Any other business must not be used in this way. Here are some reasons:

- Important items, and especially those requiring a decision, must have adequate discussion time. This is not easily provided right at the end of a meeting.
- Participants will usually be preparing to leave when the meeting arrives at AOB, which may render the meeting inquorate.
- It short-circuits the normal procedure for placing items on the agenda in advance of the meeting, suggesting that it is unnecessary.
- It allows issues that may have far-reaching consequences to be nodded through in haste, without adequate thought and debate.
- Any other business has been known to be used by less scrupulous members of organisations in order to force an issue through, thereby distorting a charity's aims and objectives.
- It can become a dumping ground for awkward subjects that no one really wants to tackle.
- It makes it difficult for the chair to manage the meeting and to stick to agreed finish times.

Pro-forma for agenda items *Please complete all sections*

Meeting title and date:

Agenda item title:

Purpose of item: *Please tick one*

    For information ☐   For decision & action ☐   For approval ☐
    For discussion ☐   For the record ☐   Other (*please explain*) ☐

Brief description (*max 40 words*)

Please indicate how much time you think should be devoted to this item:

Is there an accompanying report or paperwork? *If so, please give details*

Name/phone number of originator: ....

Please submit all items to .... no less than .... days before the meeting.

- Participants may have other appointments to attend, after the meeting, and may therefore miss matters of interest or importance, which are brought up under AOB after they have left.
- Items brought up under AOB will not be numbered and may prove difficult to minute effectively.
- If there is a 'free-for-all' approach to items being brought up under AOB, inappropriate issues may arise which, had they been known about in advance, could have been excluded or referred to a more appropriate meeting.
- Contentious or difficult issues may be brought up which can result in the meeting degenerating and getting out of control.

Any other business can be placed on the agenda but there must be some clear conditions, which are agreed and understood by everyone who attends the meeting. These conditions should be thoroughly incorporated into the protocols and general conduct of meetings.

Here is a sample set of conditions that can be adapted for use in any organisation:

1   People attending the meeting are forewarned that if anyone wants to bring an item up under AOB, they must inform the person chairing the meeting *before the meeting begins*. That means they must notify the chair or secretary beforehand, and attend not less than ten minutes before the meeting is due to begin.

2   Any item brought to the chair must have a title, brief description, purpose and an approximate allocation of time. For example:

    Title: Health & Safety
    Description: Complaint about trailing wires in training room
    Purpose: For information
    Time: 5 mins

3   The chair of the meeting can then decide at the beginning of the meeting, in consultation with the members, whether an AOB item is sufficiently important to be added to the agenda and given its own number.

4   As a general rule, the chair can advise that AOB items brought to him/her in advance will only be taken if they fall into one of the two following categories:

    a)   the item is a genuine emergency. It came to light *after* the agenda had been prepared and circulated, and must be dealt with because it cannot wait until a subsequent meeting. If it requires a decision, any relevant background information must be available, preferably in written form.

b) the item is very brief and is for information only – for example announcements about forthcoming events.

Here is an example of a chair's script, when dealing with AOB at the very beginning of the meeting.

Three items have been brought to me to be raised under AOB. Two are brief, but urgent, items for information, which will add no more than five minutes to our anticipated finish time of noon. The third concerns a potentially serious health and safety issue which shouldn't be delayed until our next meeting. If we add it to the agenda today, we can at least set the ball rolling on tackling it. It'll probably take between five and ten minutes. Is everyone happy with that? (General nods of agreement.) In that case, can you add item number nine, health and safety, to your agendas and adjust our approximate finish time to 12.15.

'Tabled' papers

Sometimes people bring papers or reports to be circulated at the meeting. These may support items already on the agenda or they may relate to an item of any other business. It is up to the chair to decide whether these can be accepted. The chair should insist that people provide papers in advance, in order to save time at the meeting. The chair could even refuse to discuss items where the papers are not available.

From the point of view of the minutes, if the meeting accepts the paper, you record that it was 'tabled'. Either put 'paper tabled' beside the heading, or mention it in the body of the minute:

A paper on current problems with the boiler was tabled by the Premises Manager and discussed.

Any paper that the meeting relied on in making any of its decisions must be filed with the other agendas and papers.

5 Assembling the minute taker's toolkit

In preparation for the meeting, the minute taker will normally have to assemble a large number of items. It is therefore not acceptable for the minute taker to be stuck in a corner with a pad balanced on their knee. Instead, you need to sit at a large table or desk next to the person who is chairing the meeting (even if other participants are in easy chairs), because you may need all of the following at hand.

Essential items

To fulfil all the roles of the minute taker you will need various items with you at the meeting. Under the headings below you will find a list of the things you must have.

What you need to get the minutes signed

- One 'master' set of the minutes of the previous meeting to be signed.
- The current minute book or file of approved minutes.
- Hand-written notes of the previous meeting (in case anyone questions the typed version).

What you need to record attendance

- A list of people who are expected to attend.
- Attendance register/signing-in book for those present (if kept separate from the minute-taking notebook).
- A list of those who have offered their apologies for absence from the meeting.
- The record of attendance for the last few meetings (in case the meeting wants to consider expelling someone for persistent non-attendance).

(See *All meetings need an attendance record*, page 80, for more information on this topic.)

What you need to do with the business of the meeting

- Spare copies of the agenda for the meeting.
- Spare copies of the draft minutes of the previous meeting and action sheets (if the latter are separate from the minutes). Spare copies of any of the papers or reports that are to be considered at the meeting.
- The minute book or minute file for the organisation/group, covering at least the previous two years (in case there is a need to refer back to previous decisions and actions).
- Copies of any correspondence received.
- Details of any actions or progress achieved since the last meeting that may be queried under matters arising.
- Dates and venue details of future scheduled meetings.
- Diary(ies) covering at least twelve months ahead.
- A copy of the constitution and/or terms of reference for the organisation/group (see *Governing documents and terms of reference*, page 43).

Other essential equipment

- Clock or watch, to record the time the meeting began, and the time it closed.
- Pens.
- A notebook or pad in which to take notes (see following section).

Items you may need

Some organisations will also require the following to be available:

- Name plates to place on the table, or name badges (see *Know who the people are*, page 20).
- Travel expenses claim forms.
- Any forms that people may have to sign – such as registers of interest or nomination papers for officer posts.
- Calculator.
- Flip chart or over-head projector.
- Spare notepads and pens for participants to take their own notes.
- Details of forthcoming holidays, including dates of local school holidays or local religious holidays.
- A gavel, for the chair to regain everyone's attention.
- Refreshments (but see *The minute taker is part of a team*, page 7).

Additional items which may be useful

- Highlighter.
- Seating plan, showing who is sitting where (see *Know who the people are*, page 20).
- Tippex.
- Background reports or papers which may be relevant to agenda items but which are not actually on the agenda.

The notepad you choose is important

Although it is part of the minute-taker's toolkit, what you write your notes on is so important that we have given it a separate section to itself.

Many minute takers use A4 refill blocks, tear-off notepads or small shorthand pads, spiral-bound at the top so that they fold over (rather than sideways). Although these are in common use in voluntary organisations we believe they are not suitable for note taking in meetings. Here are the reasons:

1   The hand-written notes of a committee, sub-committee, or any decision-making meeting constitute a legal document. Until the typed version is accepted and signed at the subsequent meeting (which may be several weeks in the future), the hand-written notes constitute the legal record that the meeting took place. They should therefore be kept safe in a notebook that has a formal status with some permanency. Its pages should be numbered so that it would be obvious if the notebook had been tampered with.

2   The sheets of paper on tear-off pads inevitably become detached from the pad, once they've been turned over. For note-taking purposes, the minute taker should not have to deal with loose sheets of paper.

3   The note taker may be asked during the meeting about something which took place half an hour earlier. It is embarrassing to have to sort through sheets of loose paper looking for the item.

4   The notepad should contain a permanent key to abbreviations used in the notes (see *Use abbreviations – but with care*, page 78). This is not possible in a fold-over pad.

5   Fold-over pads have no intrinsic value, are cheap and cheerless, and, like pens, grow legs, are borrowed, mistaken for another person's and disappear.

6. The fold-over pad in which the minute taker took notes may be used for other purposes – for personal jottings, messages, to-do lists and the like, making it even harder to keep meeting notes separate from other matters.

What sort of notebook or pad is suitable?

Every meeting which takes place on a regular basis – whether it is a staff meeting, committee meeting, general external or internal meeting – should maintain its own notebook, which is reserved for the hand-written notes of that particular meeting and for nothing else.

The notebook should be sturdy, with stiff covers, and should open sideways. Spiral-bound A4 notebooks work well because, when opened, they can lie flat, displaying two sides of A4. Even better are proper A4 hard-back notebooks with stitched rather than gummed binding.

In either case, notes from any particularly lengthy agenda item can be taken across two visible pages, making it easier to transcribe afterwards.

As stated above, each page should be numbered, so that it would be obvious if a page had been torn out. The date and meeting title should be clearly written at the top of the relevant page. A copy of the agenda should also be stapled or stuck to the relevant page, after the meeting has closed. If the meeting made any amendments to the typed agenda, these corrections can be written by hand directly onto the agenda. (Remember that for formal meetings, where decisions are taken, the hand-written notes taken during the meeting are a legal record of the proceedings.)

The first few pages may be reserved for signing attendance (see *All meetings need an attendance record*, page 80). The outside front cover should be clearly and prominently labelled, something like this:

Newtown Community Centre
Management Committee meetings

From March 10 2000 to (*insert end date when the book is full*)

Minute-taking notebook

Note takers: Jane Smith and Sue Adcock (part-time administrative workers)

See inside front cover for record of attendance from March 2000–
See inside back cover for key to abbreviations used in notes

DO NOT BORROW OR TAKE AWAY

Needless to say, this notebook should be kept in a secure place, which is known to the chair, the note takers, and any key workers involved.

Using a prepared note-taking layout

An alternative to going in with a pad of blank paper and hoping for the best is to use pre-prepared layouts for your note taking. If our recommendations regarding the agenda (see *A good meeting needs a good agenda*, page 24) are followed, you can spend a few minutes before the meeting laying out in advance your notes on the main agenda items. These help in two ways:

1 By doing some of the work of note taking before the meeting, you have less work during the meeting, and therefore more time to listen actively.

2 It helps your note taking during the meeting by giving your notes a structure, from which to transcribe the typed version (see *Plan your minutes around a framework*, page 96).

This preparation can either be hand written, straight into your notebook, or on printed sheets which are pasted in. If you are writing them by hand, allow a double-page spread for each item. A printed sheet can be pasted on the left-hand page, with the page opposite left blank for additional material. It could look like this:

Item no: Background papers: Who to introduce:

Topic:

Type of outcome expected: Decision/Discussion/Information/
Approval/Record
(*you would tick or circle the correct one in the list above*)

Set the scene:

What happened next:

Key points raised:

Decisions:

Action:

In particular, reserving specific spaces for decisions and action points helps you to identify these quickly and also to spot if there is a gap where no gap should be. Perhaps you could encourage the meeting to 'clarify' its decision at that point, or specify who will take the necessary action.

Much of the information can be completed in advance. You know already, from the agenda, who will introduce the topic, what the background papers are, and what type of outcome is expected. You can certainly guess how to set the scene, and probably make a fair stab at what happens next.

For minor items, and items for information only, you do not usually need the full version. Here again, however, any preparation you can do beforehand will make life easier during the meeting.

6 Governing documents and terms of reference

All formal meetings, and some less formal ones, work to a document that sets out the rules for how a particular meeting operates. If you don't know the rules, you don't know when you are breaking them.

Most organisations have a governing document that lays out how the organisation is run. If the organisation is incorporated as a company limited by guarantee the governing document will be a memorandum and articles of association. If it is unincorporated it will often be constitution or a deed of trust. (Whether or not the organisation is a charity is irrelevant here. Charities may be incorporated or unincorporated.)

Normally the governing document will give the most important rules about how 'general meetings' of the organisation (such as the AGM) are run, and how meetings of the management committee or board are to be run, and include things like the membership, the quorum and the notice period for meetings. If the governing document doesn't say anything about these, a limited company must follow the rules in the Companies Act.

A committee may also draw up additional rules for itself, or for general meetings of the organisation. These are often called standing orders.

The governing document, standing orders or terms of reference should be available during the meeting in case any queries arise as to the rules governing the conduct of the meetings – such as voting procedures, or the number of people necessary to constitute a quorum. It is useful to know the exact paragraph or page number where such rules are specified, so that it can be located easily. The minute taker, together with the chair, shares responsibility for ensuring that the meeting is quorate whenever decisions are taken. The minute taker may have to keep track of people's comings and goings if members leave early or arrive late.

Sub-committees and working groups

When a committee sets up a sub-committee or working group, it is usual for it to give guidance as to what the sub-group can and can't do, who its members are and what its quorum is, among other things. This document is called the terms of reference.

The difference between a sub-committee and a working group is normally that a sub-committee can make decisions on behalf of the main committee; a working group can only make recommendations, which have to go back to the main committee for approval.

It is important to be clear about this, so that when you are minuting the meeting where the sub-committee or working group reports back, you know what to write. The minutes of a sub-committee just need to be received and noted for information. It has made its decisions (and probably put them into action already), and the main meeting just needs to know what they are. There may occasionally be questions, but there should normally be no lengthy discussion about the content of the decision, provided the sub-committee has acted within its powers.

The minutes of a working group should be phrased as *recommendations* to the main meeting. If you have a good chair, they will ensure that the discussion doesn't start all over again: if people wanted to contribute, they should have put their views to the working group or volunteered to be on it. However, the main meeting does have to decide whether to accept or reject the recommendations.

Informal groups

Occasionally a group will be set up with no terms of reference or governing document. Sometimes this is because the group is thought to be too informal. Running and minuting such a meeting may be particularly difficult, as it is not always clear who is allowed to participate or how decisions are made. At other times there are no written terms of reference because the rules are thought to be obvious. With a staff meeting or team meeting, everyone in the team is obviously involved, and the decisions will either be made by consensus or under the guidance of the team leader or line manager. Even here, however, it may be worth establishing some basic ground rules so that everyone really does operate on the same basis.

Exercise

Find out which document governs the committee or meeting that you most often minute. Read a copy and make sure that you understand:

- the composition of the committee
- the quorum
- how much notice must be given of meetings.

7 How to tell if a meeting is valid

For the decisions of a meeting to stand unchallenged the meeting must be properly called, legally constituted and properly run.

If a meeting is not valid, then any decisions it takes are not real decisions. They have no legal weight. This could get you into trouble in all sorts of ways. The members may be able to mount a legal challenge. Funders may not give you your grant if you cannot prove that you have taken decisions properly. Individuals may become personally liable for taking action that was not properly authorised.

The responsibility for making sure that a meeting is valid lies with the chair, often in partnership with the chief officer of the organisation. However, as part of the team, the minute taker can make a useful contribution by:

- helping to get things right when the meeting is called;
- reminding the chair of any factors they may not have noticed or have forgotten;
- ensuring that the minutes demonstrate that everything necessary was done to make the meeting valid.

Properly called meetings

In order for a meeting to be properly called:

1   Everyone who is entitled to attend the meeting must be told that it is happening.

2   This information must be given out in good time before the meeting – for many meetings the notice must go out at least a week beforehand; sometimes the deadline is two weeks, and for an AGM it might be six weeks or more. (For more on the notice period see *Governing documents and terms of reference*, page 43.)

3   People must be told where the meeting will take place, when it will take place and what will be discussed.

Even if your entire committee happens to meet up in the pub one night, they cannot decide to have a committee meeting there and then, because the meeting has not been properly called. Nothing they decide in the pub can carry any legal weight (which is probably just as well).

Sometimes a calling notice will be sent out well before the deadline, telling people about the place and time of the meeting and asking them to notify the chair or secretary of any items they want discussed. This will then be followed (still before the deadline) by a further confirmation, along with the agenda. More often, the agenda will be prepared by the chair or secretary and sent out at the same time as the calling notice.

The reason for sending the agenda is so that people will know what is going to be discussed. If they have particular views on a matter they can then make a point of attending the meeting. This is one reason why the agenda *must* indicate not just a broad heading (such as 'Staffing'), but also the main issue(s) needing a decision (such as 'To approve the appointment of a new project worker'). If something is not clearly on the agenda that was sent out in advance, then the meeting shouldn't take a final decision about it, unless it is a genuine emergency. (See *A good meeting needs a good agenda*, page 24.)

The secretary of a committee must keep an accurate list of who is entitled to receive notice, and where to send it. Although it is often the case that a genuine mistake doesn't invalidate a meeting, it is far better to take the trouble to avoid mistakes in the first place.

Legally constituted meetings

People may attend a meeting for a variety of reasons. However, to make the meeting valid, the only ones who count are those who are entitled to participate fully in making the decisions – in other words those with a vote. (Even if the meeting normally decides things without a vote, what matters is whether people would have a vote if it came to one.)

Not everyone with a vote has to be there; the minimum number required is called the quorum. If enough people are there, the meeting is quorate; if not, it is inquorate. When writing minutes, you have to demonstrate that the meeting was quorate, in order to prove that it was a valid meeting. You must therefore separate out those people who contribute to the quorum and those who do not.

You should list those with a vote as 'present', and list everyone else as 'in attendance'. It is usual to explain why those in attendance were there. The different categories you may come across include:

Voting members

All formal committees must have named voting members. They are entitled to attend the meeting, to speak and to vote. They must be told about the meeting and they must get copies of any papers that will be referred to in making decisions. For the purposes of the minutes they may be present, absent with apologies or absent without apologies.

Non-voting members

Non-voting members are relatively rare. They often attend ex officio (because of their job). They have all the rights of voting members, except the vote, and they do not contribute to the quorum. On a school governing body, for example, the head teacher can choose to be either a voting or non-voting member.

Non-members

Non-members are people who attend the committee regularly, but have a more limited role, and no vote. They may be:

- entitled to attend and to receive papers etc. – for example as representatives of the staff or some other body;
- required to attend, as part of their work – again, particular members of staff may be told to attend all or occasional meetings;
- invited to attend whenever they wish.

Non-members may need permission to speak. They cannot vote, and do not contribute to the quorum.

Non-members may include observers who play no part in the meeting, but are there to check that things are done properly or to obtain information. For example a major funder might ask to send an observer to monitor how its grant was being spent, or another organisation working in the same field might send an observer to maintain good links with your organisation.

Guests and visitors

Guests and visitors are people who don't normally attend that meeting. They may be invited just for a particular item or part of the meeting – perhaps to give a presentation – and they may or may not speak on other items.

Co-opted members

Co-opted members do not fall into the above categories. Co-option refers to how people get onto a committee. Co-opted members are chosen by the other members, not elected or appointed by some other organisation. They may or may not have a vote, depending on the rules of the committee (and in some cases they may have a vote on some matters but not others). If they have a vote, they count towards the quorum; if not, they don't. (To find out more about the make-up of your committee see *Governing documents and terms of reference*, page 43.)

If people arrive late, they don't count towards the quorum until they get there. If they leave early, the meeting may become inquorate without them. The minute taker therefore needs to alert the chair (see *A protocol between the minute taker and chair*, page 13) and indicate in the minutes when people arrive and leave, if they are not there for the whole meeting. For purposes of showing that the meeting is valid, this needs to be in the body of the minutes, at the chronological point where the arrival or departure happened. If the meeting becomes quorate or inquorate as a result, this should also be noted, along with any action that the chair decides is necessary.

> [During the above item, Rehana Shah left the meeting. The meeting therefore became inquorate, and the Chair announced that the remaining agenda items would be discussed briefly in order to give advice to the staff, but without taking any formal decisions.]

You should indicate the actual time at which people arrived or left and the items they missed, as in the example below.

Present
Paul Ticher
Lee Comer
Gill Taylor (until 4.30pm, not present for items 6 to 11)

Properly run meetings

The running of a meeting is, of course, largely the responsibility of the chair. The chair must ensure, for example, that people who are entitled to speak have a proper chance to say their piece. People who are entitled to vote must be allowed to do so. Decisions on major items should only be made if they were on the agenda and adequate time was devoted to them. All the relevant information should be available so that decisions are soundly based.

Except in an emergency, if any of the above conditions do not apply – prior notice on the agenda, enough time or adequate information – the chair should postpone the decision until the next meeting.

The minute taker may be able to indicate in the minutes that the meeting has been properly run, by including phrases like 'after a full discussion'. If there is a vote the minute taker should not normally record who voted which way, just the totals. In other cases the minutes may simply need to indicate how the decision was reached (see *Recording how decisions are made*, page 58).

PART **THREE**

During the meeting

8 The minute taker in action

Know what is expected of your minutes

It will help you enormously during a meeting if you understand what is expected of your minutes. You will then be in a better position to follow the key points of the discussion and to take notes that will be of most use to you. The story told in the case study below will be familiar to many of you.

Case study

Jan, an administrative assistant with good word-processing skills and some shorthand, had worked at Newtown Single Homelessness Project for six months. She was asked to minute the monthly meetings of the project's development team during her induction period. The purpose of these meetings was to share information, discuss new initiatives, plan the development budget and respond to government consultative documents.

Jan was given the agenda to type at 10.00am on the day of the meeting, which was scheduled for 2.00pm. The agenda was circulated at the meeting. It looked like this:

1) Information update from 3 outreach projects

2) Proposal to merge volunteer recruitment functions with training team

3) Budget position

4) Responses to consultation paper on rough sleepers

She found it hard to follow the discussions in the meeting and she struggled with the jargon. She wasn't even sure which agenda item was being discussed as people jumped to and from different items. No one explained anything to her but they looked at her occasionally to check that she was making notes.

She wrote down as much as she could. The meeting lasted three hours and she took her notes home that evening. It took her four hours to transcribe her 24 pages of notes into six pages, which she typed up the next morning and gave to her manager.

Four days later, she received the notes back with many amendments and insertions. Jan was embarrassed, but made the corrections and again passed the minutes back to her manager. The minutes were returned two days later with another small amendment. Jan made the correction and again passed them back. They were then returned to Jan with a note asking her to copy and circulate them to all those present at the meeting and the committee chair.

Jan wondered why her manager had not commented on the quality of her minute taking. She plucked up the courage to ask her colleagues about their experiences and discovered that the process she had endured was considered normal. After three months in the post, she was told she had done well in her probationary period and that her appointment was permanent.

As she became more familiar with the organisation, she could reduce the time she spent transcribing her notes, but she still felt troubled by the endless to-ing and fro-ing of her typed minutes. She calculated that she spent an average of three hours per month taking notes at the meetings, followed by at least four hours writing up and typing them. What troubled her most, however, was that, apart from her manager, no one seriously bothered to read the minutes.

We recognise that Jan's story above is an everyday phenomenon in voluntary organisations. But the problems she encountered were not of her own making. These problems can arise because any one or more of the following factors is at work:

- Meetings are chaired badly.
- The agenda is badly constructed and uninformative.
- Participants place too much reliance on the minute taker to transform long and rambling discussions into neat summaries.
- Participants expect to see all their comments and contributions repeated in the written minutes.
- Chairs or key workers may take the opportunity to 'doctor' the minutes, to present their preferred version of the outcome.

- Different parties at the meeting attempt to re-conduct the meeting, through the process of compiling the minutes.
- Participants wholly misunderstand the purpose of minutes, expecting them to repeat the entire proceedings of the meeting.

We shall now look at some of these and other issues to help you avoid experiences like Jan's.

Spend more time listening than writing

It may seem obvious that during a meeting the minute taker should be taking notes that will eventually be written up into the minutes. However, this is not the whole story.

The fundamental point is that the minute taker should not be aiming to write as much as possible. In fact, you should aim to write the *least* amount necessary to produce the minutes afterwards. This is because the less you write, the easier it will be to extract the information you need for the minutes. Instead of discarding sheets of material that do not contribute to the finished product, as Jan did in the case study above, it is far better to avoid writing so much in the first place – and giving yourself cramp or worse into the bargain.

In order to achieve this you need to:

- have a clear idea of what the finished product will include, so that you only write what is relevant;
- understand the issues;
- learn to listen to what is going on, so that you can pick out what is relevant;
- structure your note taking so that the material goes down on paper in the most useful way;
- use judicious abbreviations and short cuts that free up your mind to get away from your notes and back to the meeting.

Your best tool in a meeting is your brain, not your pen.

Other factors which will help the minute taker include: recognition from the organisation that note taking and minute writing are skills which can be developed through training and practice; adequate preparation time (as discussed in Part Two); acceptance of the minute taker as a full, professional member of the team and good chairing (discussed below on page 56).

What do good minutes look like?

Once you have an idea in your mind of what you are trying to achieve, it then becomes much easier to decide how you can organise your work during the meeting so as to achieve it with the minimum necessary effort.

At this point it is worth having a look at what the 'ideal' set of minutes might look like. We have said above that the primary purpose of minutes is to show what decisions were made, and to show that they were made in the right way. If that is all you are doing, the minutes can be very short, as the example in Appendix A (page 154) shows.

In order to produce minutes like the example, firstly it is necessary to ensure that everyone concerned with the meeting understands what the minutes are for and, more importantly, what minutes are not designed to do. In particular, they are *not* a verbatim record of the meeting. (See *Minutes are not a verbatim record*, page 105.)

Secondly, some discipline needs to be introduced into the planning, chairing and conduct of meetings so that no undue pressure is placed on the minute taker to produce a coherent set of minutes from a random and arbitrary discussion or, in other words, to make a silk purse out of a sow's ear. Too often, people are sent on minute-taking courses in the hope that they can achieve this unreasonable aim – it is unreasonable, and it is an abdication of responsibility by all the other people involved in the meeting to put that burden on the minute taker.

Just how short can minutes be? In essence, a minute of an agenda item is that which can be written in a minute (60 seconds). Test yourself now on how many words you can comfortably, and legibly, write in 60 seconds.

How did you do? The most likely outcome is that you wrote between 20 and 35 words, possibly more, but certainly nothing like the speed that people speak at – typically over 100 words a minute.

This figure of between 20 and 35 words will be our starting point for considering what you should be aiming to write down during a meeting.

Meetings must be properly chaired

When minutes are written by hand in a book as the meeting progresses, it is (or should be) clear to everyone that the minute taker cannot just write things down as they happen. Real meetings just don't take place in a neat, manageable order. Instead, at some point the chair has to decide that the discussion has gone on long enough, and either that a decision has, in fact been reached or that people are ready to make the decision – by a vote if necessary. When the decision has been made, the chair announces what it is, and the minute taker writes it down.

Without that discipline, life for the minute taker can become much harder. If the meeting is being badly chaired, discussion may move from one topic to another without a clear break in between. The meeting may make a 'decision' then go back to the same topic later and either change the decision or add further elements – often without being clear whether the original decision still stands. People may volunteer to do things without it being clear whether the meeting has agreed that they should. Someone may assume that their suggestion has been accepted because no one argued against it, while others think that it was rejected because no one picked it up. The meeting may break up into several sub-meetings discussing different aspects of the topic.

The important thing about a meeting like this – and we have probably all experienced it at some time – is that it is not only the minute taker who is left confused. The people in the meeting don't know what has been decided either. This is serious, because they have to take collective responsibility for their decisions. A participant who thinks that a particular decision has been made may go away happy. When they find out that everyone else thought the outcome was the opposite, it will be too late to raise their objections.

This can give rise to recriminations and bad feeling, and a waste of considerable time when the topic has to be reopened at the next meeting. It is also hard for the minute taker – unless they are prepared to misrepresent the meeting – to produce minutes that demonstrate decisions being taken in the correct way.

The solution, of course, is good chairing. While this in itself could be the topic of a book, the important point here is that the chair *must* ensure that everyone present is clear when a decision has been made and what it is. The best way for the chair to do this is to bring discussion to a halt and either ask for a vote or announce what the decision appears to be, inviting people who disagree to say so. If there is a vote, the chair must specify very clearly what people are being asked to decide, or which options they are being asked to choose between.

This gives you, the minute taker, the chance to check that you have understood properly, and it should provide a breathing space when nothing new is happening, during which you can write the notes which will eventually turn into your minute of between 25 and 30 words.

You may still have to be on the ball, as an experienced chair with a familiar group of people may feel able to summarise and move on very quickly. However, the best chairs will check with the minute taker that they have had enough time before moving on. No one loses out from an opportunity to pause, collect their thoughts, rustle their papers and prepare for the next item.

Other ways in which the chair can help the minute taker and, incidentally, everyone else include:

- making introductions at the start and identifying people who enter the room late (or asking people to identify themselves);
- reminding people to speak up;
- preventing several people from talking at once;
- announcing clearly which item is under discussion and reminding people to stick to the topic;
- pointing out if there are relevant background papers;
- taking charge if it becomes clear that the agenda needs to be changed, for whatever reason – perhaps because a discussion has raised an important item which needs its own separate slot, or because the order needs changing when key people arrive late or need to leave early;
- reminding participants about confidentiality and identifying confidential items in good time.

Recording how decisions are made

Many voluntary organisations are very vague about the actual process of decision making. Often, it is unclear exactly how decisions are made; they just seem to 'emerge'. This is not necessarily a bad thing. You do not need to call for a formal vote on everything, provided everyone is happy that decisions are still being made properly.

When making a decision without a vote most organisations seek a consensus. Strictly, this means that everyone is of a like mind. However, in a meeting it more usually means that everyone feels happy that they have participated fairly in the discussion leading up to a decision, and they are prepared to let the decision stand without challenging it, even if they personally would have decided differently. Typically, the chair will say something like 'Well, I think we've decided to go ahead with the project. Is everyone happy with that?' If no one speaks up, the decision stands. The minute taker can record this as a decision. If someone says 'No', the chair might ask for a vote, or they may try to persuade the objector to accept the majority view. You should be guided by the chair on whether to minute the objection or not.

Other ways of making a decision include 'by acclamation' (when people call out 'aye' or 'nay', 'yes' or 'no') and 'by show of hands'. A show of hands is different from a vote. Provided there is a clear majority, the chair just announces the decision without counting. Anyone at the meeting can ask for a 'poll' or vote if they disagree with the chair's judgement. If you are minuting an AGM or other large meeting, you may want to indicate how the decision was made. For a smaller meeting, the only time this is necessary is when there is a vote.

If you are recording a vote, you should include the full result, including abstentions (those who do not express a view either way). Everyone who has a vote must:

- vote for (or in favour)
- vote against or
- abstain.

If you give all three totals, then it is possible to see immediately how many people with a vote were present (to demonstrate the quorum), even if they didn't all actually vote. (Note that the chair does not need to ask for abstentions, unless they are unsure who has voted and who hasn't. Anyone with a vote who doesn't vote for or against has automatically abstained.)

❝ My Chair wants me to record which way people have voted. Is this correct? **❞**

We believe it is not good practice to record who voted which way, since it detracts from the general principle that committees act collectively. Once the vote has been taken, it does not matter which way specific people voted. However, some organisations do record who voted which way, and it is certainly not illegal to do so. The Charity Commission leaflet CC48 says that the minutes should show 'who voted and how'. This could be read to mean that you must record which way people voted. However, from discussions with the Charity Commission it is clear that they are not adamant about requiring a record of which way people vote.

Some chairs may use the words 'unanimous' which means that everyone with a vote agreed, or '*nem. con.*' (*nemine contradicente*), which means that no one disagreed, although some might have abstained. You don't have to use the same words in your minutes if you think people won't understand, although you may find that your chair prefers their own wording.

What you must be careful to avoid, when taking minutes, is assuming that a decision has been made, either because the decision was suggested by someone important or because you happen to agree with it. If in doubt you should check with the meeting. You could ask 'Was the Chair's suggestion accepted?' or 'Shall I minute that as a decision?' This may be particularly important if you feel that someone is trying to railroad the meeting into a decision the majority is not happy with. By indicating what you are considering noting down as a decision, you give people the chance to speak out against it.

Remember that deciding not to do something is still a decision. You must record the fact that the lack of a decision was deliberate, not an oversight. So your minute might look like this:

Refurbishment of hall

The proposal to repaint the hall and replace worn-out curtains was discussed at length.

Decision: It was agreed not to pursue this at present due to lack of funds.

❝ Our meetings are very formal. Everything is 'proposed' and 'seconded', with 'points of order' being raised. Is it true that I have to minute the names of the proposers and seconders and so on? **❞**

If this is how people actually want the meeting conducted, then you normally do have to give the names of proposers and seconders. However, this type of procedure is really only applicable to large, formal meetings such as some AGMs. Originally it came about as a means of making sure that meetings were properly run. Now, it is much more often used to intimidate people who don't understand the procedures, and usually hinders free participation. Good chairing is a much better solution.

See *Minuting an annual general meeting*, page 141 for details of how to minute these formal procedures.

If you miss something, you can ask for clarification

If a meeting is being averagely chaired, you may well find that most of the decisions and actions are agreed clearly enough, or are obvious to everyone, but some confusion still lingers. At this point, if you have your protocol agreed (see *A protocol between the minute taker and chair*, page 13), you should be able to interrupt proceedings and ask for clarification: 'Could I just check the decision? Jim will have a further conversation with the Projects team before going ahead with the application, but the committee has given the go-ahead if that meeting is positive?' or 'Jane offered to invite the local paper to the Fun Day. Was that agreed?'

If they say 'yes' to this last question, the minute could show the outcome as a decision, 'The meeting asked Jane to invite the local paper to Fun Day' rather than having in the body of the minute the accurate, but much less helpful, 'Jane offered to invite the local paper to Fun Day', which leaves the decision hanging.

When all else fails, you can fall back on the all-purpose, 'How would you like that minuted?'. Obviously this cannot be over-used, but it can be a very effective way of forcing a meeting to face up to the fact that they don't actually know what they have decided, or haven't made it clear to everyone.

Other times when you may need to ask for guidance from the chair include:

- when someone asks for a particular point to be specifically minuted, or not minuted;.
- when you feel that a discussion should be recorded as a confidential minute but the chair has not given any guidance;
- when the meeting makes two (or more) mutually contradictory 'decisions';
- when the meeting makes a decision which is clearly impractical – such as expecting someone to take action while they are on holiday;
- when the meeting tries to make a decision which is not within its powers: you may have to minute it as a recommendation rather than a decision.

9 Minutes that are written during the meeting

Much of this part of the book is about gathering information during a meeting which will subsequently be turned into minutes. However, it is important not to forget the alternative: writing the minutes during the meeting itself.

Here we give the procedure for writing the minutes directly and once only, by hand, into the organisation's minute book.

1 The minute book must be a hardback, stitched, sideways opening A4 book with lined, blank pages.

2 The cover must show the name of the organisation and the particular meeting, and identify the book as the minute book (e.g. 'Management Committee Meetings Minute Book').

3 The spine of the book should be labelled with the dates and period covered by the minute book (e.g. March 1999 – March 2001).

4 The pages should be numbered.

5 The date, place and time of each meeting should be written at the top of a new left-hand page.

6 The members sign in as being present.

7 Those in attendance sign in underneath (see *How to tell if a meeting is valid*, page 46).

8 The agenda comes next. It may be hand written using black ink or (if typed) pasted in. Any written reports or papers accompanying the agenda may be filed separately, but must be identified or annotated, for example as follows 'Progress Report on outreach project. Agenda item 4, Management Committee meeting, 11 March 2001'.

9 The minute taker notes the time the meeting begins directly into the minute book (e.g. 'The meeting began at 7.35 pm').

10   Nothing is written in the minute book while discussion takes place. Instead, at the end of each agenda item, the chair summarises the decision. The minute taker then turns this summary into suitably formal draft wording and reads it out. When it has been agreed by all present, the minute is written by hand clearly and legibly using black ink, directly into the book. (This should take no more than one or, at the most, two minutes of time.)

11   Immediately after the minute for the last item on the agenda has been written, the minute taker, or the chair, may again read aloud what has been written. If there are any final corrections they are made there and then, and initialled.

12   The minute taker then writes 'The minutes of this meeting were read and approved as a true and accurate record'. The chair then signs underneath.

13   The minute taker writes in the time the meeting closed.

If members require copies of the minutes for their own records, the relevant pages of the minute book can be photocopied or typed out and circulated.

It will be apparent that, with the above method, there is no need to circulate draft minutes, no need for preliminary checks and no awkwardness about minuting corrections.

In addition, there is an effective discipline in having to agree the text of the minute at the time, rather than later. Participants are obliged to agree the text, and therefore to act as a group, rather than as a disparate collection of individuals with their own particular axes to grind.

The entire process of writing the minutes will take no more than a few minutes per agenda item, which is considerably less than the awkward and long winded process which has been brought about by reliance on word processors.

This method of taking minutes is, thankfully, alive and well. At least half the charities and voluntary organisations in Britain have no offices, no computers and no paid staff. Many of them follow the above procedure without problems and without challenge to the authenticity or legality of their minutes.

The procedure is eminently suited to a variety of types of meetings in larger voluntary organisations with paid staff. It is quick and easy, and serves as a permanent record of the work of the particular group.

Here are some examples of the types of meetings that could adopt this procedure:

- informal working groups
- task groups
- staff meetings
- interdepartmental meetings
- discussion groups.

There may be situations where the above method can be supplemented by short reports (rather than minutes) of a meeting. For example, a staff meeting could maintain its own hand-written minute book, but where it has discussed matters which others need to know about, a short report written in everyday language, rather than minute language, could be circulated. It is much more likely to be read than the typed minutes!

Case study

A real-life voluntary organisation with five paid staff and three volunteers uses this system for minuting team meetings. The minutes are hand written directly into a book, with action point details, and are read back at the end of the meeting and signed off as correct. The book is kept in a prominent place and every member of the team – particularly those who were absent – has to initial and date the page to confirm that they have read it. For a small organisation it's an excellent way to ensure that everyone knows what has been agreed and what their tasks and responsibilities are, without imposing a big burden on the minute taker or anyone else.

A variant on this method that is worth considering is to write the notes up on flip charts for everyone to see during the meeting. If people understand from the outset that the minutes will only consist of the contents of the flip charts, possibly tidied up a bit, but with nothing added, then it is their responsibility during the meeting to check that they are happy with what has been recorded. This approach is particularly useful where the minute taker is an active participant in the meeting, and for recording wide-ranging discussions where the actual decisions are few and far between.

Thanks to modern technology, some people now have the option of typing a rough version of the minutes straight onto a laptop computer during the meeting, to be tidied up afterwards. The main advantages of this are:

- legibility – the minute taker has no need to be embarrassed by their handwriting;
- speed – many people can type more quickly than they can write;
- availability – if the minutes are on computer they can be printed out and circulated more easily than when they are written by hand.

However, this is not the whole story. Minutes prepared in this way are emphatically not the same as minutes written into a book.

- The chair cannot sign them on the spot.
- Participants in the meeting cannot see that what is being typed is the same as what has been read out.
- There is no way to prove that the final copy of the minutes that is circulated is the same as what was read out during the meeting.

Using a laptop may have much to commend it. It certainly helps the meeting to focus and offers a massive reduction in the minute taker's workload after the meeting. However, we would recommend that the resulting minutes should be treated as though they had been typed up afterwards, in terms of the procedures for approval and signing set out in *Minutes must be signed*, page 91.

10 Note-taking skills and techniques

It does not follow that a person with word processing skills can also take intelligible notes during a meeting, and yet many managers assume that the two skills are identical. Taking notes during a meeting is highly skilled work that, like most other skills, develops best with practice.

How much to write

Some people take pride in their ability to write very fast – 40 or more words per minute is not uncommon amongst experienced minute takers – but it is not advisable over prolonged periods. People who attempt to write very fast throughout the meeting are risking their health. In order to write fast over extended periods of time, it is necessary to grip the pen very tightly – it is this that leads to repetitive strain injury, tennis elbow, arthritic fingers and writer's cramp. Tolstoy, Dickens and all the great writers of long novels suffered from these ailments, as do many minute takers today.

Twenty to thirty-five words per minute is the best speed, with the proviso that every minute of writing is balanced by five minutes of listening. It is an instructive fact that the average length of a minute in traditional hand-written minute books is between 20 and 35 words, for – as we saw above – this is exactly what can comfortably, and legibly, be written in 60 seconds. It is also an enlightening fact that anything and everything can be summarised in an average of between 20 and 35 words.

Everything can be summarised in 20–35 words

The film of Billy Elliot
Billy Elliot, the son of a Tyneside miner, discovers he is a talented dancer. He overcomes his family's resistance, wins a scholarship to ballet school and makes a successful career as a ballet dancer. (34 words)

The plot of Anna Karenina
Anna Karenina, an aristocratic woman in nineteenth century Russia, leaves her husband and child to live with her soldier lover in exile. She is tormented by her disgrace and finally commits suicide. (32 words)

From Ashbrook Parish Council records
'It was agreed that four dwellings be built at the southern end of John Brown's field to provide permanent accommodation for four stonemasons and their families.' (26 words)

From Oldtown Village Residents Association (1994)
'It was agreed that a Carnival sub-committee be formed to oversee the planning and preparation of the Oldtown 1995 summer carnival.' (21 words)

If between 20 and 35 words is the length of the minute that you are aiming to produce at the end of the process, it is a waste of time and resources to write down everything that happens during a meeting. This was demonstrated in the story about Jan on page 53.

We recognise that many voluntary organisations – and especially those with paid staff – have come to expect minutes that are more detailed than is strictly necessary. While not wishing to condone this practice, we will look at some ideas and techniques that will help you to improve your note-taking skills even where additional information is required.

Three note-making techniques

There are three main techniques, and we would recommend that you try out all three in different situations. You may find that one method suits you above the others, or that each method lends itself to different types of agenda items.

1   30-word summaries, written in 60 seconds

Where a discussion is complex, and covers a great deal of content, we would suggest between 5 and 10 minutes of active listening, interspersed with summaries of 30 words written in 60 seconds (see *Hearing is not the same as listening*, below and *Writing summaries*, page 70).

2   Using a pro-forma

These are prepared before the meeting, and can be customised for each agenda item. We would advise that they are either pasted into a notebook, or the book is marked up in advance (see *Using a prepared note-taking layout*, page 41).

3 Mind map/spider plan/spray diagram

Some people are immediately comfortable with this technique while others may have to practise a little. This method of note taking is taught to students because it aids note taking in lectures and helps with thinking and study skills. Try it out and see for yourself (see *Mind mapping*, page 73).

Don't forget that planning and preparation can help you to take appropriate notes. Some of the main ways, which are all discussed elsewhere, are:

- by helping you to identify the important points in a discussion through a better understanding of the agenda and the issues behind it (see *Understand what is being discussed*, page 18).
- by cementing your relationship with the chair (see *A protocol between the minute taker and chair*, page 13).
- by devising an appropriate set of abbreviations (see *Developing and using your own abbreviations*, page 79);
- by writing in advance anything that you know will have to be recorded (see *The notepad you choose is important*, page 39).

Hearing is not the same as listening

There is a profound difference between hearing and listening. Hearing is a mechanical process – that is, one can hear words and discussion without listening, and without taking anything in. It is rather like being able to read a page of text without taking it in. At some time or another, we have all read an article, or a page of text, and, having arrived at the end, realised that not a word of what we've read has gone in. We have to re-read it, but this time we have to concentrate on what we are reading in order to understand it.

The parallel with note taking is exact. The ears are hearing, the hand is writing, but the information is not being taken in. It is perfectly possible to write and hear at the same time but it is quite impossible to write and listen at the same time. Listening requires full attention. But the moment we switch from listening to writing, the focus of attention alters and we no longer listen.

Note takers who try to write down as much as possible are hearing, instead of listening. People in this situation will say that their minds begin to wander, yet they succeed in covering sheets of paper with notes. Some report emerging from a long meeting with plenty of notes, but with little or no memory of the discussion.

The key to good note taking, therefore, is listening. You need to be familiar with the jargon that is being used, need to understand what people are talking about and you must listen very attentively. Every now and then, you can stop listening in order to write a sensible summary of the discussion so far (see *Writing summaries*, page 70). And at that point, you are concentrating on what you are writing, knowing that it will make sense and will be intelligible not just to you but to anyone else who might wish to look at the notes.

Listen with understanding

Regrettably, many workers in the position of Jan in our case study (page 53) believe that if they were able to take shorthand, or if they could write much faster, their problems in minute taking would be solved. They fondly believe that a verbatim repetition of the meeting would prevent subsequent disputes and eliminate the need for corrections to their typed versions of the minutes. But this is not the case.

By concentrating on trying to write everything down during the meeting, minute takers are postponing the process of making sense of the proceedings. They believe that understanding will come when they read their notes later. But if the minute taker hasn't listened to and understood the discussion, they cannot produce a coherent summary for the minutes.

Readers may remember their lessons in primary school when they had to produce a summary or précis of page of text. It was impossible to produce a sensible précis unless one understood and absorbed the full text – hence the term 'comprehension'. If understanding does not take place during the meeting, it is unlikely to jump off the page and emerge fully formed from your notes afterwards.

> **❝** I can't understand what some of the members of the meeting are saying – sometimes because of the jargon they use, but sometimes because their accents are hard to understand or they mutter. **❞**

If it's a question of jargon that everyone else understands and you don't, your best hope is to mug up on it in advance. When a meeting is in full swing, with the best will in the world people will be reluctant to make allowances. However, if some people are using jargon that most of the meeting doesn't understand, draw this to the attention of the chair. The members who don't understand are being disenfranchised and excluded just as much as you are.

When people have strong accents or mutter, this is only a problem for you if they are saying things which have to be recorded. If you are focusing on the decisions and action points, you do not normally need to record individual contributions. So once again it is more a matter for the chair to ensure that everyone's contribution is being heard and taken into account. If you miss a decision or action point you must ask for it to be repeated.

Writing summaries

If you have established how many words you can write in 60 seconds – let's say it is between 20 and 35 words – you should aim to write that many words in each short burst of writing. An important skill, which comes with practice, is judging when to stop listening so that you can 'drop out' of the meeting for long enough to write these short notes. So, for instance, the discussion has gone on, around the houses and backwards and forwards for ten minutes. You've listened, attentively, to the discussion but have not attempted to write down what's been said. But at a convenient point – perhaps when someone starts repeating themselves – you can take your 60 seconds to jot down your summary.

Here is an example. The subject of the agenda item discussion is local authority grant aid. First we give the verbatim record.

Jim: I've seen the agenda for the Council's Policy & Resources Committee next week and there's something on it about a possible standstill – or even cut-backs in grants to voluntary organisations.

Jane: Yes, we knew this was on the cards, but they've not consulted with any of the groups they're funding. I met Sue Jones from the After

School Club yesterday in the supermarket and she said that their councillor who sits on her management committee – you know Councillor Nelson – told her that the Council would be facing some hard decisions. She took it as a very strong hint that he was talking about across-the-board cuts. And she also said – and I thought this was very interesting – that he seemed to be saying that nothing was really settled. They're probably just waiting to see whether there's going to be a fight back or an outcry of some sort. If there is, they might back off. That's the impression she got.

Graham: Well, we can't just let them do this without at least talking to us. Don't they realise what it will mean to us, and to our clients? We'll have to give them a fight back.

Jim: We can't jump the gun like this. And we can't act alone. We're all in this together, don't you think?

Narinder: It could really put their backs up if we go in, guns blazing, before anything's been decided. I think we should be tactical and diplomatic at this stage. I think we should find out what other groups have heard and if it looks serious, we ought to consider doing some quiet lobbying of our own councillors before the meeting. And then if the decision at Council is bad for us, then we should mount a campaign. Maybe talk to other groups and have a joint press release or something, but only after we've spoken with our own councillors – and maybe the officers in the Council.

Graham: I agree, but we'll need to get cracking pretty quick.

Jane: I'm seeing Councillor Whybrow tomorrow. She's helping to launch this safety campaign group I'm on. I could mention it then.

Graham: I think we should write formally to both the councillors on our management.

Narinder: What about ringing them both up, and then following up with a letter?
(Discussion continues on the merits and de-merits of writing or speaking to councillors… People are beginning to repeat themselves – as yet no decision.)

And here is a summary – in note form – of the discussion so far.

P & RC discussing 29 Jan grant cuts for local vol. orgs. Not decided. Ideas: make a fuss? Alert councillors quietly to likely impact of cuts before they make decision?

In order to produce the above summary, the note taker has listened attentively and formalised the naturally conversational tone of the discussion. The exact words of the participants have not been quoted, but the note taker has produced an effective, objective summary of the key points.

Further discussion took place before the group reached a decision. Narinder's suggestion was raised again, and the group settled on a plan to contact their councillors and council officer in order to make them aware of the damaging impact of any cut to their grant. They also decided that if their council went ahead with the cuts, they would organise an emergency group meeting with a view to mounting a big campaign, possibly in partnership with other affected groups.

While the group continued to chat about what kind of campaign they could organise, the note taker wrote the following summary in 33 words.

> Contact by 19 Jan 2 councillors – Richards and Khan + council officer Sue R. (A = Jane) re: impact of possible cuts. If Council goes ahead, emergency meeting to organise campaign – with others similarly affected?

From these notes, the final version of the typed minute was written as follows:

3.0 Newtown Local Authority Grant Aid   For decision

The information about possible future cuts in grant aid to voluntary organisations, due to be considered by Newtown Council's Policy & Resources Committee meeting on January 29, was discussed.

Decision: It was agreed that Cllr Richards, Cllr Khan and Sue Roberts, Council Officer, be contacted by phone or in person before Jan 19 to alert them to the damaging impact of any cuts in our grant aid.

Action: **Jane Hughes**

Time: Immediately, no later than 19 January.

Decision: It was also agreed that, should the Policy & Resources Committee meeting decide to cut our grant aid, an emergency Management Team meeting would be arranged with a view to mounting a campaign against these cuts.

Action: **Management Team.**

Time: Diaries to be kept clear for this eventuality.

Mind mapping: a different way of note taking

Nine out of ten people, when given an A4 pad and asked to take notes, will hold their pen poised at the top left hand corner of the page and will start writing. They will write fairly continuously, gradually covering the page. After ten minutes or so, they will have to turn to the next page to continue writing. When the discussion has finished, they will have succeeded in representing, graphically, how the time has been filled. The comments made during the discussion will be noted on the page in the order in which they were made. When these nine note-takers then take their notes to the word processor, they find that they have to re-order their notes to arrange them into a summary that is appropriate for typed minutes. And in the process of re-ordering, they draw arrows backwards and forwards through time, connecting up the disparate elements. This is time consuming, and totally unnecessary.

The tenth person starts by putting the subject of the discussion in the *centre* of the page. As the themes and points emerge during the discussion, the note taker can group them together.

Drawing a mind map

A group of people in a room was asked to suggest items to pack for a Mediterranean summer holiday. Their suggestions were noted directly onto a flip chart, as a list:

sun cream	credit cards	tickets
novels to read	swimming costume	insect repellent
tea bags	sunglasses	sun hat
evening clothes	shorts	camera
passport	kettle	guide book
currency	address book	

There is no logical sequence in this list. It is random, as you might expect from a wide range of people, in the same way that people's comments during meetings are random. The note taker has faithfully written things down in the order in which they were said, without making any logical connection or grouping between the items.

Contrast this with the diagram of notes below. This form of note taking defies the tyranny of time, allowing the points to be grouped together logically, rather than in the random order in which they were suggested.

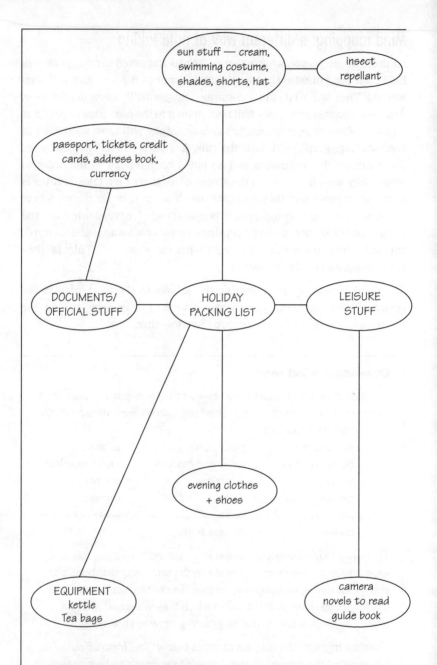

This note-taking technique is known as a 'mind map', or 'spider plan' or 'spray diagram'. See also *Further reading*, page 167.

Here is another example of a mind map, taken from a real meeting where people were discussing what to do about queues in a busy advice centre:

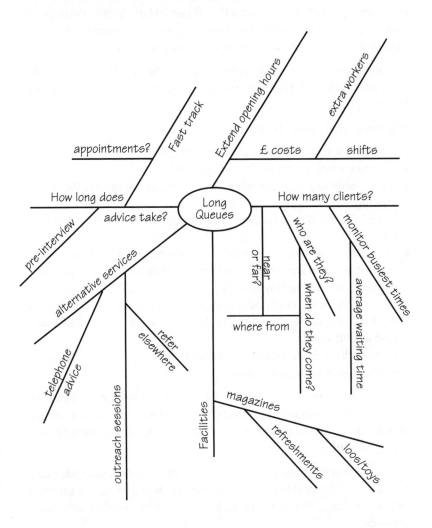

The above mind map can easily be converted into a written summary of the ideas, grouping them together under the general themes that emerged during the discussion. If a decision had been reached, it can be circled or starred.

Do not use shorthand or tape record the meeting

Although at first sight shorthand might appear to be an advantage, most experienced minute takers do not find it particularly useful. We hope we have made the case by now that there is no merit in writing down more than is necessary – which shorthand encourages you to do.

Another key reason to avoid shorthand is that the notes taken during the meeting must be legible and intelligible not only to the note taker but also to others.

The reasons not to use shorthand are therefore:

- It leads to verbatim or near verbatim records.
- It takes too long to transcribe and type out.
- It will inevitably require a lot of time to edit into some sensible minutes.
- The likelihood of another person being able to read the shorthand is nil.
- The person who takes shorthand is not listening, but hearing, concentrating on converting words into shorthand, and therefore is not summarising the proceedings.
- Until the minutes are signed and approved, the notes taken during the meeting form the legal record. Problems will arise if they cannot be read or understood.
- If the note taker is taken ill, or goes on holiday, no one else can transcribe the notes into minutes.

If you know that you are going to be able to transcribe your notes straight away, and *if* the minutes are in effect dictated to you by the chair at the end of each item, you might get away with using shorthand. Otherwise it should be avoided.

Tape recording meetings is an even worse option. Some people feel that a recording is unavoidable because it is the only way they can be sure that they will not miss something important. In practice, however, this rarely succeeds:

- A two-hour meeting will produce a two-hour tape. If you have to listen to the whole thing and write up the minutes it is just extra, unnecessary work.
- On a tape it is even harder to hear what people are saying than it is in the meeting, especially if they mumble or talk across each other.

- On the tape you get no visual clues to help you identify who is talking.
- If you are having difficulty following the sense of the meeting, there is no guarantee that you will be any the wiser after listening to the tape. It might just be a disorganised meeting, or you might have done better to spend the time preparing beforehand rather than struggling afterwards.
- Even if the recording is intended just to back up the notes on specific items, you still have to find the relevant part of the tape and hope to make sense of it when you do.
- Arranging the tape recorder and microphone, and checking or changing the tape when it runs out, distracts the minute taker from listening to the meeting.

Occasionally a minute taker resorts to tape recordings because they are concerned that people will challenge the accuracy of the minutes, or they fear that senior colleagues will insist on changing the minutes afterwards to reflect their wishes, not the decision of the meeting. As a result, the minute taker feels that they need hard evidence to back up their notes. These situations are, of course, highly regrettable and the minute taker should not have to cope with them. Neither situation is a good reason to tape record the meeting. While it might give the minute taker peace of mind, it is hard to imagine these tape recordings being used as evidence except in the context of a major row. In that case, other factors would almost certainly come into play, including eyewitness evidence from other participants in the relevant meetings.

A better solution is to concentrate on producing short, accurate minutes. The shorter the minute, and the more it focuses on the decisions only, the less scope there is for anyone to challenge it – especially if the minute taker has been able to clarify the decisions during the meeting. It is also harder to change an explicit decision, and more likely that those attending the next meeting will notice, and challenge, any falsified record. Ultimately, it is the responsibility of the meeting to accept or reject the previous minutes. (How long you would choose to stay in a job that made life so difficult for you is, of course, a different question.)

> **❝** I was trained to use a pencil when taking shorthand, but I've been told not to use a pencil when I'm taking notes at meetings. Why not? **❞**
>
> It's true that a pencil is best suited to writing shorthand, but the hand-written notes of meetings constitute a legal document until the minutes of the meeting are accepted and signed. Pencils must not be used because the notes can be falsified very easily.

Use abbreviations – but with care

While shorthand is not usually a good idea – as discussed above – it is perfectly acceptable to use abbreviations when taking notes to cut down on the amount of writing you have to do, especially where it is repetitive.

However, you should be careful not to use this as an excuse to write down more than your summary of between 20 and 35 words. Instead, you write the summary in less time and return your attention to the meeting that much sooner.

You must also ensure that:

- you use each abbreviation consistently to mean the same thing;
- you don't use so many abbreviations that the meaning gets lost;
- the abbreviations are spelt out in full in the typed minutes;
- the notebook being used incorporates a key to their meaning. This is best kept at the back of the minute-taker's notebook. (There are some abbreviations which are in common use, such as e.g.; i.e.; asap. Obviously, these won't need to be in the key.)

Initials, jargon and acronyms and a key to their meaning

It's important to remember that the notes taken by the minute secretary during the meeting are not a secret code, intelligible only to the note taker. Each organisation will generate its own in-house abbreviations and these may change over time, so it is important to update and maintain the key to their meaning.

Similarly, many of the outside organisations with which voluntary organisations deal are known by their initials, but these will change over time, so it is always important to spell them out in your typed minutes and to incorporate their meaning in the key.

Here are some examples of initials and acronyms that may be incomprehensible, unless explained, to new employees and committee members, and to future generations:

The National Lotteries Charities Board (NLCB) was in 2001 renamed 'The Community Fund'.

In the same year the Further Education Funding Council (FEFC) and the Training and Enterprise Council (TEC) were amalgamated as the Learning and Skills Council (LSC).

Statutory funding agencies also come and go, each generating their own acronyms. Do you recognise UP, SRB, ERDF, RECHAR, P4?

A key also helps to avoid misunderstandings. How many completely different meanings do you know for CP or IT? The possibilities for IT include Intermediate Technology, Intermediate Treatment, Industrial Tribunal and Information Technology. The fields of health, education and social welfare are particularly rich with initials, jargon and changing acronyms. Here are a few we have seen in minutes with no explanation: SNTA, SEN, ADD.

Developing and using your own abbreviations when taking notes

In addition to jargon and acronyms, there is the question of the minute taker using customised abbreviations. Where common phrases and terms appear regularly in your minutes, you can develop your own abbreviations to encompass these.

Here are some possible examples:

IWA   =   It was agreed

MWD   =   The matter was deferred

PMA   =   The minutes of the previous meeting, held on X date, were approved and signed

DONM   =   Date and time of next meeting

There are many more you can develop. Readers who are skilled in text messaging may be able to apply their skills in note taking. We have included a sample of abbreviations, using initials and symbols, in Appendix B, page 158.

11 All meetings need an attendance record

All meetings – even small internal meetings – *must* have a procedure for participants to 'sign in' their attendance. Proof of attendance may not seem particularly important at the time, but it may subsequently prove to be so.

Case study

This is a true story. A new worker from a northern charity was sent to represent her charity at a consultative meeting of similar organisations held in central London and scheduled to begin at 9.30am. She therefore travelled down the night before and stayed in a London hotel. Her travel and overnight expenses amounted to over £250 for which she had receipts. Of the twenty-six people who attended only two knew each another. Introductions at the beginning of the meeting were made verbally. When the minutes of the meeting were sent to her charity her name was not among those listed, but she insisted to her employer that she had been there. Her charity tried to sack her for theft/gross misconduct, on the basis of there being no proof that she actually attended the meeting.

For the example in the box, a simple signing in procedure would have avoided any doubt.

Such examples are not unusual. In many cases, individuals attending meetings will be claiming travel and subsistence expenses, attendance allowances, loss of earnings or will be attending meetings outside their regular employment, as part of their public duties. Proof of their attendance is frequently required for audit and other purposes.

The fact that someone's name appears as 'present' in the typed version of the minutes does *not* usually constitute conclusive proof of their attendance. The normal rule is that signed minutes are *prima facie* evidence of what happened (and who was there) – in other words they are taken to be true unless anyone challenges them, in which case additional evidence would be needed. A signature on an attendance sheet is far better additional evidence than the possibly unreliable memories of other people who were present.

The minute taker will normally be expected to operate the signing-in procedure. Our recommended procedure is different depending on whether the meeting is a regular one with a fixed membership, or one with a more fluid and unpredictable attendance.

Regular meetings with fixed memberships

At regular meetings with a named membership – such as committee meetings, staff meetings and the like – the following procedure is recommended.

The register of attendance, which members sign, should be either in a separate, permanent book, or in the front of the minute-taker's permanent note-taking book (see *The notepad you choose is important*, page 39). The names are printed or typed vertically down the left-hand column, as in the example below. The title of the organisation/meeting is typed or written along the top. Members sign in, under the appropriate date, against their name. Apologies for absence must also be noted. If a person does not attend, and fails to offer an advance apology, the minute taker marks them as 'absent'.

Newtown Community Centre – Finance Sub-Committee meetings Register of attendance – March–November 2001				Quorum: 4
	Meeting date	Meeting date	Meeting date	Meeting date
Members	11 Mar 01	17 May 01	13 Sept 01	14 Nov 01
	Signature	Signature	Signature	Signature
John Waters	*John Waters*	*John Waters*	*John Waters*	*John Waters*
Miles Cann	Apols recd	*Miles Cann*	*Miles Cann*	*Miles Cann*
Kevin Bligh	*Kevin B ligh*	*Kevin B ligh*	Absent	*Kevin B ligh*
Kay Levene	*Kay Levene*	*Kay Levene*	*Kay Levene*	Apols recd
Jen Kaur	*Jen Kaur*	Apols recd	*Jen Kaur*	*Jen Kaur*
Sue Carter	*Sue Carter*	*Sue Carter*	*Sue Carter*	*Sue Carter*
Meena Singh	*Meena Singh*	*Meena Singh*	*Meena Singh*	*Meena Singh*
Jon Richards	Jon Richards	Jon Richards	Jon Richards	Absent
Jane Smith	*Jane Smith*	*Jane Smith*	Apols recd	*Jane Smith*

You can also calculate the quorum for these meetings and write it on the sheet, as shown, so that there is no delay in working it out each time.

The method set out here has the following advantages:

- There is a permanent record of attendance.
- There is permanent proof of attendance.
- An individual's attendance record is available at one glance, rather than having to wade through previous minutes.
- There is visible evidence (and proof) of a quorum for those meetings which require a quorum to be present.

All governing documents and terms of reference should contain a clause which requires members of committees to attend meetings or, if they are unable to attend, to give their apologies in advance of the meeting. Constitutions usually also contain a clause requiring committees to make certain provisions if members fail to attend and fail to give their apologies. This clause usually says something like:

> A member of the Management Committee shall cease to hold office if he or she is absent without the permission of the Management Committee from all of their meetings held within a period of six months and the Management Committee resolves that his or her office be vacated.

The signing in procedure that we have recommended above provides an at-a-glance record. If a member is recorded as 'absent' for the two previous meetings and fails to attend the third, it is vital that the minute secretary draws the chair's attention to this fact at the beginning of the third meeting, after everyone has signed in. In this way the organisation complies with its constitutional rules. The chair may then decide to add the matter to the agenda of the third meeting, in order to obtain the committee's agreement to any action to be taken.

One-off, occasional or open meetings without a fixed membership

An attendance register should be passed around for every person to sign.

The format should be as follows:

Newtown Tenants' Association – Residents' Meeting
6 September 2001

Please sign in below

Full name (Please print)	Signature	Contact details

If the minutes are to be typed up after the meeting, the list of people attending should be copied from the attendance register. The original sheet or book in which people signed should be kept with the master set of signed minutes.

❝What happens if people can't sign their name?❞

If someone attending a meeting is physically unable to sign their name, but can put a mark against their name, with or without help, they should do so. If they can't do this, someone else should sign for them (making it clear that they are signing on their behalf).

PART **FOUR**

....

After the meeting

12 What to do next

Procedures to follow

We have already discussed the procedure for writing minutes directly into a book during the meeting. In that case, the minute taker has very little to do after the meeting, apart perhaps from photocopying the minutes for distribution, filing relevant papers and putting the minute book away securely.

Life is very different for a minute taker in an organisation that relies on minutes typed up after the event. The procedure we recommend for this is as set out in the list below. The flow chart on page 89 summarises the procedure.

1   Transcribe your hand-written notes into a typed version, as soon as possible after the meeting, making sure that every page says 'draft' in the header or as a watermark.

2   Get the draft, typed version checked by a key worker or the chair.

3   Circulate the draft version to everyone who was entitled to attend, together with a reminder of the date of the next meeting, at which these draft minutes will be signed.

4   Print one 'master' set of these draft minutes without their 'draft' heading. This is the set of minutes to be signed, which will be filed, after being signed, in the 'master' minutes file (or minute book) and kept in a secure place.

5   Make sure that approval/signing of these minutes is near the beginning of the agenda of the subsequent meeting, normally at item two or three.

6   Everyone attending the subsequent meeting will have had an opportunity to read the draft minutes before the meeting begins. Before being asked to approve the minutes, participants must be given the opportunity, by the chair, to propose any corrections. If the chair and the meeting agree to someone's proposal to make a correction, this should be written in black ink by hand on the master set and initialled. The minute taker can make the correction but the chair should initial it.

7   The chair then signs every page of the master set of minutes, in full view of the meeting.

8   Write in your notes that the minutes were approved. If there were any corrections, make a note of the exact changes that were written onto the 'master' copy. Any amendments must be matters of fact, rather than of opinion (see *Minutes are not a verbatim record*, page 105).

9   Do not re-issue a 'corrected' set of minutes or photocopy the signed 'master' set for circulation to members. Every committee member has a right to view the 'master' minute file. They may also, of course, write any corrections that were made onto their own draft copy by hand.

10 File the 'master' set of signed minutes in its safe place, together with the agenda and the attendance register that meeting.

You can either file the agendas and papers separately from the minutes or you can file agendas, papers and minutes all together in the same file. If filed separately, what matters is that they are cross-referenced and easy to identify. Ensure that they are filed by year (usually the organisation's financial year) – e.g. Minutes of Management Committee Meetings 1 Jan – 31 Dec 2000, next to the file marked Agendas and Reports for Management Committee Meetings 1 Jan – 31 Dec 2000.

" How can I use Word to put 'DRAFT' on every page? **"**

The best way is usually to use a 'watermark'. Go to Help (press F1), select Index and type 'watermark' as a keyword, then follow the instructions. In earlier versions that do not support watermarks, you should use the header to put 'Draft' prominently on every page.

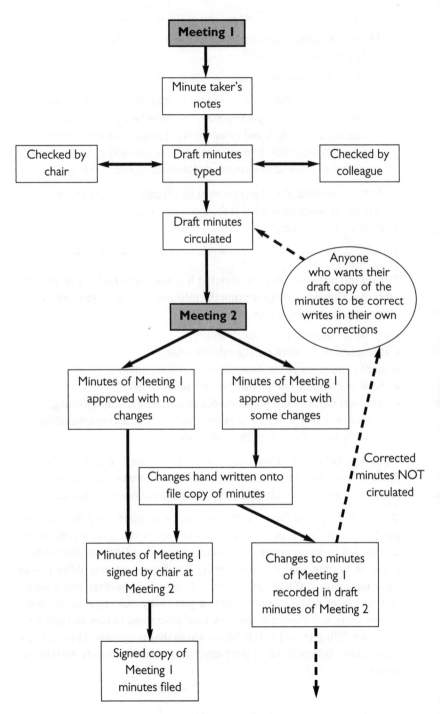

> **❝** What happens if someone won't accept the minutes, even if the majority agrees them? **❞**
>
> You should minute their objection. For example:
>
> > The minutes of the meeting held on 11 May 2001 were approved as a correct record and signed by the Chair. However, James Wilson objected to Minute 3 and asked for his objection to be recorded. In his view the decision to make redundancies was only to be followed up after efforts had been made to obtain emergency funding.
>
> At the same time, the objection must be recorded by hand on the minutes to which they refer, in the same way as an agreed correction, before they are signed.

Typing the minutes after the meeting has introduced a host of possible problems. Compared with writing the minutes once, and once only, into a minute book, the results are that:

- the whole process takes much longer;
- it is much more work for the minute taker;
- there is more scope for disagreement and argument;
- there is a temptation for the minutes to be longer;
- approved minutes are not available until the following meeting, which can cause problems if people need to take action immediately on the basis of the committee's decision.

What was, before word processors, a simple, authentic and totally legal process has become a complicated and increasingly inauthentic procedure, but one which many organisations cannot do without.

You should type up the minutes as soon as possible after the meeting. Ideally do it the same or the next day. The sooner you do it, the more you will be able to rely on your short-term memory to fill in any gaps in your notes, or to help you decipher anything written unclearly. After two or three days, you will have to rely almost entirely on written notes which may no longer make so much sense. If you really can't type up the notes immediately, you should at the very least scan them to pick out any gaps that need filling in and to tidy up anything that is unclear. This will also help to keep things fresh in your mind when you eventually do type the minutes.

Until the master set of minutes is approved and signed, your hand-written notes, together with the signing-in record, constitute the only proof that the meeting actually took place. They therefore have a legal status and they must be kept in a safe place.

❝ My manager always wants to add things to the minutes that didn't happen in the meeting. What should I do? **❞**

Ideally, you should refuse, but this isn't always practical. In the end it is not your responsibility. The subsequent meeting should spot the fraud and get it corrected. In order to protect yourself, you may well want to hang on to your notes, so that you can show that you didn't record the matter in dispute. Another approach may be to make a point of checking your notes of the meeting at the time – especially if the chair is sympathetic. Then it is that much harder for your manager to argue that they are wrong.

There are times when it is legitimate to make additions. If a decision is invalidated by subsequent events, it is appropriate to say so. You should put the comment in square brackets. For example:

[The planned meeting of the Finance Committee subsequently had to be postponed owing to the rail strike.]

Minutes must be signed

The main and over-riding purpose of minutes is to prove that meetings take place. They alone provide proof that an organisation conducts its affairs responsibly and legally, with full accountability for its decisions and actions. The minutes must therefore be kept for all time, in a secure place. Such proof provides essential evidence:

- that the organisation is complying with its constitution and with all legal requirements;
- that the organisation is accountable for its decisions and actions to its members, users, the Charity Commission, partners and funders;
- that its decisions are taken by the people who are authorised to do so (hence the significance of proof of members' attendance and proof of a quorum);

- that the management of its finances is subject to appropriate controls;
- that decisions and actions undertaken by the organisation's staff or volunteers have the necessary approvals.

With modern computer technology, anyone can fabricate a set of minutes for a meeting that did not take place, but without a procedure for accepting and signing the minutes there is no proof. For any committee or group with decision-making powers it is not enough for the next meeting just to accept the minutes. The procedure for accepting and signing minutes is absolutely critical.

The most important elements are:

1   Only one copy of the minutes should normally be signed. (It has been known for a superior body to require an additional signed copy for its own records. In most cases it is unnecessary.) All other copies of the minutes should say 'draft' on them.

2   The minutes should be signed in the presence of the meeting that agrees they are correct.

3   Changes must be written in immediately, by hand, and initialled by the chair.

4   If the minutes are loose-leaf, every page should be numbered and initialled. (Space for this can be incorporated into a standard footer on the word processor.)

These procedures may seem heavy-handed for the less formal meetings. In practice, for example, few organisations ensure the chair initials every page of loose-leaf minutes, but it really should be done. Guidance on the law for school governors from the Department for Education and Skills, for instance, says: 'The minutes of each full governing body meeting must be kept in a book and, following approval by the governing body, signed by the chair at that or the next meeting to confirm that they are accurate. Alternatively, the minutes may be kept on numbered loose leaf pages, each of which must be initialled by the chair'.

Even for less formal meetings it is good discipline for a 'master' copy of the minutes to be identified and to be signed by the chair. If you haven't been signing minutes in the past, you cannot go back and have old minutes signed, but do start signing them from now on. If it was important enough to minute, it might be important enough to need proof later.

When the minutes are written directly into a book during the meeting, the chair only needs to sign the minutes for each meeting in one place, at the end, regardless of the number of pages the minutes occupy. It would be instantly apparent if a page were torn out and it would be impossible to substitute a false or inaccurate page.

“ Our chair signs the minutes when I send them to him at home. He sends them back to me and I photocopy them and send them to everyone in time for the next meeting. Is that correct? **”**

No, it's not correct. The members of the committee must have an opportunity to approve the minutes before they are signed. That is why they must be signed at the next meeting and why members must be asked if the minutes are an accurate record. The chair signs on behalf of the meeting.

13 How to lay out minutes

In order to provide evidence and proof, the typed version of the minutes (or the hand-written version in a traditional minute book) should contain the following:

- The name of the organisation.
- The name of the meeting (e.g. Fundraising Committee).
- The venue (and full address, if not obvious) where the meeting took place.
- The full date (including the year) of the meeting.
- The time the meeting actually began.
- The names of the people present who were entitled to vote.
- The names of any other people who attended, and why they were there.
- An indication of when people came and left if they arrived late or left early.
- Details of any apologies for absence received, especially if there is no separate attendance record.
- The name of the person who chaired the meeting.
- The agenda items that were discussed and a record of the decisions made.
- The time the meeting closed.
- The date and time of the next meeting, if it is already known.

Most of these are either legal requirements, or specifically recommended by the Charity Commission. Many of them are needed in order to prove that the meeting was valid. For example, the venue, date and time can be matched against the calling notice to show that the meeting was properly called.

Even for an informal meeting you should only leave out any of the above items if you are absolutely sure that there is a good reason.

Putting the date and time of the next meeting allows anyone picking up the minutes for one meeting to see when the previous meeting was (from the approval of its minutes) and when the next meeting was supposed to be. They can therefore trace the whole sequence of meetings forwards or backwards from that point.

It is not necessary to specify who took minutes, although this is often done. Technically the minute-taker's identity is irrelevant, because it is the meeting which is responsible for agreeing the content of the minutes. However, if you are present, then your name should appear among those in attendance, along with the reason – minute taker. In other cases you may want people to know who took the minutes, perhaps so that they know who to get extra copies of background papers from.

Most of these items will appear in a standard layout at the beginning of the minutes, as shown in the example in Appendix A, page 154. After that follow the individual minutes for each agenda item. It is conventional to put the time the meeting finished and the date of the next meeting at the end, just before the space for the chair to sign.

In the example in Appendix A, note that the people 'present' are the members of the committee – those who have a vote, plus occasionally a non-voting member – while those 'in attendance' are the people who were present but did not have a vote. In less formal meetings without a fixed membership you would just have a list of those present.

❝ My manager wants me to put people down in four categories: present, apologies, absent and in attendance. It seems rude to put people down as absent ❞

There may be good reasons for showing which members did not turn up – for example to help in determining the quorum, or to spot people who have a history of absence. However, we prefer a separate signing-in record (see *All meetings need an attendance record*, page 80).

You do not have to spell out the reason for members being there; they are there by right. Their names should be listed vertically. For everyone else, you do need to explain the reason for their presence (partly just for information, partly so that people reading the minutes can judge who might have had an influence on the decisions made).

> **❝**Is it correct to minute someone's apology for being absent if the apology was received after the meeting?**❞**
>
> Normally you would not do this. You might make an exception if the apology was received late merely because someone forgot to pass it on. Someone who wanted to give belated apologies should really give them to the next meeting, when they can be minuted under matters arising.

We also recommend that you should have a standard footer at the bottom of every page, as shown in the example. This should include:

- the title of the meeting;
- its date;
- a running page number and total pages (usually in the form 'page X of Y');
- space for the chair to initial.

Plan your minutes around a framework

Each minute (in other words the record for each item on the agenda, or each part of a longer item) should follow a standard framework although, with experience, you will find that you can vary this a bit to cope with material of different kinds.

Some parts of the framework are essential; others depend on the way the minutes will be used and the people who will be reading them. In the list below, the essential elements are marked *.

  *1 Start with a helpful heading. Normally this will be the same heading as shown on the agenda.

  *2 Set the scene. Did the meeting receive a proposal or a report, and what was the bare outline?

  3 What happened next, in general terms? Was it discussed, were questions asked? (Or is it written up somewhere else?)

  4a If it was a report, did additional information emerge in answer to questions or during the discussion?

  4b If it was a proposal, what were the main arguments for and against? You must summarise them, rather than quoting everyone's contribution.

  *5a What were the decisions?

5b   Do the reasons for the decisions need to be recorded?

*6   Who has to take action? What must they do? By when?

You *must* record what the issue was, what was decided, and any action to be taken (*). It may be appropriate to condense or leave out entirely points 3, 4a, 4b and 5b.

Elements 1 and 2 can, in effect, be written in advance. If you are using a prepared note-taking layout you can fill these in as you prepare it (see *Using a prepared note-taking layout*, page 40).

During the discussion you must be on the look out for decisions and action points – for elements 5a and 6. You may want to reserve a special place on your layout where these are grouped together. Decisions should each be written in your notes as a summary of between 20 and 35 words. You may be able to record action points in even less but make sure you note the full details. Instead of:

> **Decision:** IWA to lobby Council over proposed cut to our grant.
> **Action:**   Pete.

your notes should say:

> **Decision:** IWA to lobby Council over proposed cut to our grant –
> particular reason: they have just paid for extension to
> building – daft if we now can't run it.
> **Action:**   Pete to write letter to local councillors and grants officer by
> 24 June, followed by meeting if possible.

(Note: IWA is an abbreviation for 'it was agreed', see *Use abbreviations – but with care*, page 78).

That takes care of the beginning and end of the minute, and it might be all you need. Note that element 5b – reasons for decisions – has been incorporated into the notes on the decision. Using the framework, the final minute for this example might read:

7b. Proposal to cut Council grant

> The meeting discussed information from the director that rumours
> of a possible cut to the grant next year appeared to be true.

> **Decision:** It was agreed to lobby the Council over the proposed
> cut to the grant. The main basis of our argument would
> be that having just paid for the extension to our building,
> it would be inconsistent for the Council to deny us the
> funds to operate it.

> **Action:** Pete Williams to write a letter to the local councillors
> and our grants officer, by 24 June, and to try to arrange
> a follow-up meeting with them.

If, however, this is an item of major concern, and you feel that the minutes should give it greater weight, you could consider whether to include additional material. Perhaps the three main issues that came up in the discussion were:

- Was the rumour really true? How reliable was the source?
- This wasn't the first time the council had tried to pull this trick, and committee members were getting angry about it.
- If we complained, would it jeopardise the money for a new staff post being negotiated with a different council department?

The discussion almost certainly did not take place in a neat, ordered way. If people were angry they might have said quite a few things that shouldn't appear in the minutes anyway; they may have gone off at a tangent; they may have half discussed something, gone on to something else, then returned to the first issue.

Your note taking will have dealt with most of that. You will have tried to make your notes concise, but you still have to do some editing. You may have written a summary of 20–35 words on a point that appeared important but later turns out to be irrelevant, so you can discard it altogether. Another summary will turn out to have missed a point that appeared minor but later came back and influenced the decision.

Your expanded minute of the discussion above might then look like:

7b. Proposal to cut Council grant

> The meeting discussed information from the director that rumours of a possible cut to the grant next year appeared to be true.
>
> In a detailed discussion, the meeting satisfied itself that this was a serious possibility and considered the likely effects on other funding areas if the matter was taken up.
>
> Members expressed their disappointment that this was not the first time the Council had appeared to change its funding decisions without consultation and at short notice.
>
> **Decision:** It was agreed to lobby the Council over the proposed cut to the grant. The main basis of our argument would be that having just paid for the extension to our building,

> it would be inconsistent for the Council to deny us the
> funds to operate it.

Action: Pete Williams to write a letter to the local councillors
and our grants officer, by 24 June, and to try to arrange
a follow-up meeting with them.

This framework has to be used flexibly. You may find that a lengthy
session needs to be broken up into several sections of discussion followed
by decision/action; discussion followed by decision/action. Or there may
be a discussion that requires minuting, even it does not lead to a decision.

Remember that it is always possible to ask the meeting, or the chair, for
guidance in how to minute a particular item. You may be able to check
your summary during the meeting – which is much better than struggling
afterwards with something that you didn't quite understand. In
particular, if you feel that the reasons for a decision need to be minuted,
try to check that your understanding of the reasons is the same as that of
the meeting.

Number your minutes and lay them out clearly

Minutes are a document that is designed to be used in practical ways,
rather than to be read and enjoyed. This means that the layout and
numbering must help the readers to:

- identify different sections;
- recognise different types of material;
- pick out decisions and action points quickly;
- find what they are looking for easily;
- refer back to previous items easily and unambiguously.

You should:

- use meaningful, informative headings;
- emphasise the headings (using bold or larger type) so that people can
  see them more easily;
- use indentation to differentiate between different types of material
  (such as decisions);
- draw attention to decisions and action points;
- leave a gap of one line between paragraphs and at least one line
  before headings;
- use a clear numbering system.

Headings

Many people just use the headings from the agenda as the headings for the minutes. This has the advantage that people can easily check the outcome of an item they are interested in. However, it may not always be informative enough for the minutes.

Think of the heading as fulfilling the same function as the headline in a newspaper: it encapsulates the story in the fewest possible words, so that the reader can decide whether they want to go on and read the full text. If they don't, then just by reading the headline they get a rough idea of who, what, where and when. (Why and how are more often in the detail.) The headings in minutes need not be quite so elaborate, but they do the same job: helping the reader to decide whether they are interested in the item.

For example, you may be working from an agenda that says:

3) Staffing (20 minutes)

   a) To decide whether to create the post of office manager.

(For decision)

   b) To appoint a Management Committee member to the Job
       Evaluation Panel.   (For decision)

When it comes to the minutes, it might be better to have:

3. Staffing

   a) Creation of office manager post
       The proposal to create the post of office manager was discussed
       in detail … *(and go on as discussed below)*

   b) Job Evaluation Panel appointment
       Robin Jones was appointed as the Management Committee
       member of the Job Evaluation Panel.

Note that in each case the heading really explains the topic 'Creation of office manager post', not 'Office manager' (which could be about the person, not the post), and 'Job Evaluation Panel appointment', not 'Job Evaluation Panel'.

It is unwise to diverge too much from the order and numbering of the agenda without a very good reason. Occasions when this might be a good idea include:

• When the discussion takes place in a different order from the agenda (perhaps because a relevant person arrives late or leaves early), especially if later decisions turn out to hinge on the earlier discussion.

- When an apparently simple item develops into a more complicated debate, which makes more sense broken up into separate sections.
- When additional items get added to the agenda in an emergency.

If the numbering and/or order differ significantly from the agenda, it is important to point this out in an aside.

[This item was taken early because the Treasurer had to leave for another meeting. Items in the minutes are numbered in the order they were discussed, not as they appear on the agenda.]

[Because this item covered several areas, it has been broken into separate sections and subsequent agenda items renumbered in the minutes.]

If you number the minutes differently from the agenda you should take care to repeat the wording of the agenda item in your heading description so that readers can clearly relate the minutes to the agenda.

Decisions and action points

There are several different ways to draw attention to the key features of minutes – the decisions and action points. The main options are to emphasise them either in the text, through the use of separate short paragraphs or bold type, or through their location at the end or the side of the item. In the minutes of informal meetings, where the minutes are very short anyway, the use of emphasis in the text is more likely to be appropriate. Except for very short items in informal minutes, it is always better to put the decision itself into a separate paragraph so that it stands out even more clearly. For formal meetings, it is usually better to put decisions and agreed actions in separate paragraphs at the end of the item.

If you want to emphasise a decision in the text, it is quite common to make the verb bold: 'The meeting **agreed** ...', 'It was **decided** ...', 'The budget was **approved**.' If you want to do this, be as consistent as possible; don't start off doing it then forget half way through. Your minutes might look like this:

Photocopier

It was **agreed** that the photocopier is near the end of its useful life. **Brenda** will ask the rep. to come in for a preliminary discussion before next week's meeting.

Recycling

The build-up of boxes of paper while we wait for a collection was discussed, especially in view of the health & safety issues.

It was **agreed** that **William** would ask if we can use the old store room in the basement for paper awaiting collection.

A more formal minute might look more like this:

3. Office manager post

The proposal to create a post of office manager, was discussed in detail.

Decision: The post will be created as quickly as possible.
Existing staff will be able to apply alongside external candidates.
Pending the job evaluation, the salary will be on the same scale as project managers.

Action: Deputy Director to report back on progress at next meeting.

In the past, when people used typewriters, a common practice was to have an action column down the right-hand side of the page. This would contain the initials or name of anyone who was required to do something to implement a decision in the text. With word processors, and the (not always welcome) possibility of further editing after minutes have been drafted, life is much more complicated if you try to reserve a narrow column on the right for action reminders. It is better to draw attention to action points either by using one of the techniques above, or by preparing a separate action sheet.

Action sheets

An action sheet pulls together all the actions agreed at a meeting and lists them, with the names of the people who have to act, and any deadline. The advantages of an action sheet are that:

- it can often be drawn up and circulated straight after the meeting, without waiting for the full minutes, so that people can get straight on with their jobs;
- at the next meeting it can be used to check quickly whether the actions have been carried out.

Against these benefits must be set the extra work involved on the part of the minute taker, both in preparing the action sheet and circulating it. It should, in theory, be possible to rely on people at the meeting who agree to do something making an accurate note for themselves of what they have agreed to do. See also *Uses and abuses of action sheets*, page 138.

If you do circulate an action sheet you must make it clear that it is based on the *draft* minutes. Anyone taking irrevocable action on the basis of the action sheet alone – initiating disciplinary action, for example, or committing the organisation to a contract – could be running a serious risk. They would be much better off double-checking their action directly with the chair or someone else who was at the meeting.

Numbering schemes

Clear numbering is important, and you can use sub-headings with their own numbers to show when items are related (for example 3a, 3b, 3c, etc.). However, don't get too elaborate, as the readers will end up confused. It is usually better to stick to just two levels if possible. If you must use a third level, because the material is genuinely complicated and the extra level really helps, a common convention is to make use of Roman numerals (i, ii, iii, iv, etc.). However, many people are only familiar with the first few of these. Once you get up to even relatively low numbers like vii, viii and ix you may begin to confuse rather than help, while xlix gets most people scratching their heads. It may be better to:

- break the item up into several separate items, each with their own two-level numbering;
- re-organise it so that you have a larger number of second-level headings;
- abandon numbering altogether for the lowest level and use bullet points instead. (People can refer to the third bullet point in item 7b, for example.)

Most minutes are numbered starting from 1 at each meeting. For most purposes this is fine. However, some committees – such as finance or personnel committees – meet very frequently, and deal with issues where referring back to previous minutes may happen a lot. It may become confusing if item 3 on the minutes of 5 October deals with the same topic as item 3 on the minutes of 25 October.

In these cases, an alternative is to use a system where the minutes are numbered consecutively throughout the year. The first meeting might have 13 items, numbered from 01/2001 to 13/2001. The minutes of the next meeting would then start with 14/2001. (Sometimes the year is put first, and may be abbreviated to the last two digits. The first three minutes of the year would then be 01/1, 01/2 and 01/3). As well as enabling individual items to be unambiguously identified, this system makes it very clear if the minutes for a particular meeting are missing, as there will then be a gap in the numbering.

Even if the minutes for each meeting start from 1, it may be worth considering numbering the meetings themselves. This is particularly valuable for formal management committee or board meetings. In this case, the first meeting of the year would be 1/01, 1/2001 or 2001/01 for example. This number can then be used to relate background documents to the meeting. A report to be considered as item 3 of the third board meeting of 2001 might then have, in its header: 'Board 03/01 Item 3'.

❝ Should I number 'apologies for absence' on the agenda if it will make the numbering in the minutes wrong? **❞**

This is acceptable. The numbering of the minutes may fail to match the numbering of the agenda for all sorts of reasons. As long as people can see clearly what is going on, it doesn't matter.

14 The content of minutes

Minutes are not a verbatim record

Minutes of meetings should not record what people said. As we have pointed out elsewhere in this book, the primary purpose of minutes is to prove that meetings take place and to record the decisions.

Voluntary organisations have meetings in order to act collectively, and to conduct their affairs in the name of the organisation, in order to serve its aims and objectives. (The organisation's constitutional rules and governing document spell this out very clearly.) In other words, the individuals involved act on behalf of the organisation, not themselves. Who specifically said what at a meeting, is therefore irrelevant. Unless people feel that a meeting has been improperly conducted, they are bound by the outcome, and share equal responsibility for it, regardless of their own personal view.

What matters and what must be apparent in the minutes, is the meeting's collective responsibility for:

- activities undertaken in the name of the organisation;
- its decision-making procedures;
- the overall management of its affairs.

It is therefore inappropriate for the minute taker to attribute comments to named individuals. The only time this does not apply is if the person making the contribution has some special standing which genuinely gives their views particular weight, for example 'The Treasurer's concern over the uncertainty behind the income figures was noted'.

If a discussion is taking place about an important subject, and if it appears appropriate to include in the minutes some of the key points, you can do so. In this example, the agenda item says:

Newtown Community Centre's bar opening hours policy

For discussion (10 minutes)

To consider whether current opening hours should be re-arranged or extended in the light of quiet times and very busy times.

Your minute might read (in part):

The following points were made:

- that to extend evening opening hours beyond 10.00pm at weekends might cause neighbourhood disturbance;

- that the income from the bar was declining with current closing at 10.00pm;

- that the volunteers already stay late to clear up and shouldn't be asked to work later;

- that the situation should be monitored and reviewed.

Note that in the above example, the comments are not attributed to individuals. However, some members of the committee may feel aggrieved that their points were not included in the minutes. It could be argued that the minute taker has chosen to include some comments rather than others because of a personal bias, opening up the possibility that the minutes are not as objective as they should be. When it comes to the next meeting, you might be asked to make corrections along the lines of 'The minutes don't include Sam Jones' contribution to the discussion'. Such changes should, in any case, be resisted, but the argument is better avoided altogether.

Within reason, the fact is that the less there is written in the minutes, the more objective they will be.

❝ The Committee that I minute insists on very full minutes. They want to see everyone's contributions written up and they especially want me to write down who said what. I know this isn't necessary, but they say I'm wrong and they're right. **❞**

You're right! Encourage them to read this book, and others listed in *Further reading*, page 167. Point out the length of time it takes to write detailed minutes, and ask them which of your other duties they would like you to drop.

An alternative and rather better minute for the above item might be written as follows:

> The advantages and disadvantages of extending weekend evening opening hours beyond 10.00pm were discussed very thoroughly. No decision was made, but the situation will be kept under review.
> (28 words)

It should be noted that the second version demonstrates that the committee is taking the matter seriously. It accurately and objectively summarises the proceedings without selecting one point over another. No member should be aggrieved, because no member's comments are singled out over another's. Rather than repeat the points made during the discussion, the minute restricts itself – quite properly – to the outcome. And, in the process, it is summarised in less than 30 words, and is also brief, clear and accurate.

66 People frequently insist that their contributions should be minuted. They say 'I want this minuted' – especially when there's an argument and they don't agree with the decision that's being made. What should I do? 99

Asking for a disagreement to be minuted does not absolve anyone from responsibility for the decision. Meetings act collectively, and if it was agreed by a majority then everyone at the meeting is equally responsible. The only genuine grounds for objection are if the decision is being taken illegitimately – for example if the meeting is not quorate – or if the meeting is not allowed to take that kind of decision. Otherwise, the person who objects has to live with it, or resign from the group.

It is the chair's decision, not the minute taker's, whether an objection should be minuted. The chair may decide to allow the objection to be minuted, out of courtesy. You should therefore look for guidance from the chair rather than obey an instruction from the person making the objection.

For much of the routine business at meetings, it is usually unnecessary to give the detail of how a decision was reached. Provided you follow the framework, give a useful heading and set the scene, phrases like the following will normally suffice:

A full (or 'wide-ranging', or 'lengthy') discussion took place.

All the options were discussed.

Several options were proposed and fully (or 'thoroughly') discussed.

The text of the decision can then be written underneath.

If you do decide to list the points made, you may want to consider saying something like 'Among the points made were ...' or 'Points made included ...'. In this way you are demonstrating that you are not claiming to have mentioned every point made by every contributor.

> **"** People frequently insist that I don't minute what they are about to say. Can they do this? **"**
>
> Yes. There are any number of reasons why people don't want their comments minuted, and their reasons should be respected. They may be speaking about something 'off the record', sharing a confidence, making potentially libellous comments (which the chair should stop, anyway). In any case, you are unlikely to be recording individual comments in detail.

Long discussions need not have long minutes

There is an understandable human temptation to feel that because people are talking in a meeting something needs to be recorded for the minutes. This is not necessarily the case. Here we summarise some of the occasions when the minutes do not have to cover what happened in any detail.

Presentations and talks

It is not necessary for the minute taker to summarise a presentation or talk, especially if a paper version of it accompanies the agenda, or if handouts are tabled at the meeting. The minute taker merely has to ensure that the paper version is clearly identified on the agenda and on the minutes, and safely filed after the meeting with the agenda. The minute can then be written as in one of the following examples:

A presentation by X on (*insert title*) was received and noted.

X was welcomed to the meeting and gave a presentation on (*insert title*).

If the presentation was followed by supplementary questions and answers, you can add 'Discussion ensued and it was further noted that ...'

Meetings that stray from the agenda

The purpose of minutes is to record decisions and actions agreed by the meeting. You can ignore anything that is clearly not relevant to the topic under discussion, such as gossip and interesting but irrelevant information.

A bigger problem occurs when the meeting takes a decision that is not related to any item on the agenda. A formally constituted committee, sub-committee, or steering group can generally only make decisions on items which have been included on an agenda sent out in advance of the meeting. This gives all members (including those unable to attend) an opportunity to give their views. The only exceptions are genuine emergencies and very minor items. Therefore any decisions taken on major, non-urgent items that do not appear on the agenda cannot be binding and thus should not, in principle, be minuted.

If someone introduces a strand of debate which does lead to a decision, you should point out to the chair that this is not on the agenda, and get them to say whether you should minute it. If they decide that you should, give it a separate item number and heading in the minutes and state that it arose during the discussion, to explain why it doesn't appear on the agenda:

4. Summer festival

During the discussion on the Christmas fête it was proposed that the society should hold a summer festival. Because of the short time-scale, the Chair ruled that this should be discussed.

Decision: It was agreed to build on the success of the Christmas fête by holding a summer festival on the third weekend in June.

Action: Secretary and fundraiser to convene a planning meeting within two weeks.

If the chair decides that the item cannot be minuted they should explain this to the meeting. If the meeting then wants to pursue the matter it should appear on the agenda for the next meeting (and this may be an action item, to ensure that the issue doesn't get lost). For example:

5. Report on refurbishment of premises

The completion of work to refurbish the premises was noted. Discussion ensued on further areas of work that will be required within the next five years.

Action: Premises Officer to present costed proposals on future refurbishment to the next meeting.

If an informal meeting has been convened without an advance agenda – for example, a working group without specific terms of reference or procedural rules – anything it discusses may be minuted.

Meetings that are entirely 'for information'

Some organisations have regular meetings between different departments to share information about their respective areas of work. These information-sharing meetings are often long, and many people find them a waste of time. There are often better ways to share information.

There are situations where everyone needs to know something. The problem with relying on a meeting is that, inevitably, someone will be unable to attend. (How often have you heard the excuse 'I didn't know – I wasn't there when everyone was told!'). Even those who are present may mis-hear things. It is far better to use more direct methods of communication.

See *Information Management for Voluntary and Community Organisations* (details are given in *Further reading*, page 167) for suggestions on other ways to share important information.

If information-sharing meetings do, nevertheless, take place they are often tedious to minute and it is hard for the minute taker to know what to record. It can be argued that such meetings do not need to be minuted. Instead, this is a clear case where those presenting information should be asked to provide a very brief written summary in advance, and participants should be encouraged to take their own notes of those matters that relate to their areas of work, rather than relying on full minutes for the details.

Case study

A well-known training organisation holds a regular series of information-sharing meetings for the freelance trainers who occasionally run its courses. At one meeting, some of the trainers present complained that other trainers had not attended, and suggested that attendance should be compulsory. This, and a few other individual views, appeared in the 'minutes', with no indication of whether they had been agreed by the meeting or whether action would follow. The resulting outrage from those who felt they had good reasons not to attend damaged the organisation's reputation, and a lot of senior management effort was needed to resolve matters. A short report on the meeting that distinguished between factual information that was being shared and discussion points (or that left out the discussion altogether) might have been far more productive.

When to record the reason for a decision

There are some situations, usually concerning non-routine, financial or personal matters, in which it may be necessary to include specific reason(s) why a particular decision was made. This need could arise for a number of reasons, including:

- to prove that a decision was not taken arbitrarily;
- to lay down a principle for similar decisions in the future;
- to show that you have been fair to any individuals involved.

Take a look at this example:

5. Proposal to apply to the National Lottery for funds to refurbish the Church Hall

A full discussion took place on the need for refurbishment and on possible sources of funding. Concern was expressed that Lottery funding derives from individual gambling, which is unacceptable to many members of the congregation.

Decision: It was resolved not to apply to the National Lottery because its funds are derived from gambling.
It was further resolved that if no suitable sources of grant funding are available, consideration be given to the possibility of organising some local fundraising activities.

> **Action:** Rev. Michael Smith to investigate and report back to the
> next meeting.

This minute taker thought it important to record the specific reason – in this case the involvement of gambling – in the text of the minute, because it touches on a wider policy matter. The decision may, in fact, set a precedent for this church's approach to fundraising. To future readers of the minutes, the decision not to apply for funding to the National Lottery may have appeared perverse had the minute not specified the reason for the decision.

If the reason is specific to the decision, it should be included with the decision although, as in the example, it may also appear in the minute of the discussion. Clearly, in this case, it was a big issue.

Where individuals are being discussed, it is often necessary to record the reasons for a decision, especially where the decision goes against them:

> The committee considered John Baker's application for extended unpaid leave.

> **Decision:** The application was turned down because it is essential that the membership database he is developing be ready no later than June. He is welcome to re-apply once it is installed and running satisfactorily.

15 Minute-writing skills

There are particular skills involved in writing minutes – both in the style in which you write and the words you choose. This chapter gives you some guidance on how you can develop these skills to produce minutes that are clear and suitable for their purpose. We shall look at:

- avoiding a personal style;
- choosing the right words for different jobs;
- checking your facts and figures;
- writing short sentences;
- when to start a new paragraph;
- bullet points.

Write clearly, but impersonally

Minutes are not an exercise in creative writing. Minutes are not supposed to be interesting to read. They are not for budding writers to try to use the widest possible vocabulary. The more creative the language, and the more faithful it is to the speech patterns of the contributors, the more open the minutes are to being misinterpreted.

Avoiding spoken styles

Here is an example of a minute-writing style that tries to combine creativity with faithfulness to people's comments:

> Jan suggested that the users' newsletter should be redesigned to make it more attractive to read. Jim noted that no one had complained to him about the design. In fact, he'd had many compliments about it. Eric highlighted the potential costs of a redesign. Jan reiterated her conviction that the design had stayed the same for a long time and was beginning to look tired and old-fashioned. Jan's suggestion was thought to be worth further investigation.

The above style of writing minutes makes several cardinal errors. It mixes and matches the verbatim with the attempt at creative writing; note the four different ways of writing 'said' – suggested, noted, highlighted and reiterated. It also faithfully follows the chronological order in which the comments were made. It follows a narrative structure – trying, in other words, to reflect the sequence of events and the flavour of the discussion. It attributes comments to the individuals and personalises them. It is potentially misleading because it is not clear whether a decision was actually taken. Someone said 'It's worth further investigation'. The rest of the group probably nodded reluctantly, before moving on to the next item on the agenda. The minute taker has faithfully written down 'worth further investigation'.

This is how it should be written.

> A discussion took place on whether the users' newsletter should be redesigned.

> **Decision:** It was agreed that research be undertaken to establish whether there is a need for a redesign and what the associated costs would be.

> **Action:** **Jane Smith**

The exact words of the decision were not actually spoken, but the minute is accurate, clear, objective – and short.

Using the passive voice

In order to be objective, minutes often come across better in the passive, past tense. This means that they are as untouched as possible by subjective interpretation. And this is why good minutes are dull, impersonal, objective and often uninformative about what actually happened.

You will almost certainly recognise the passive voice, but for those unfamiliar with the terminology of English grammar, here is an example to illustrate the difference:

> **Active voice used in everyday speech**   The car driver swerved to avoid a cyclist, mounted the pavement and hit the dog. (*Active voice, personalised to the car driver.*)

> **Passive voice, used in formal writing**   The dog was hit by a car, which mounted the pavement after swerving to avoid a cyclist. (*Passive voice, impersonal and objective.*)

Discussion takes place in a conversational, active speech pattern. When people speak to each other, as they do in meetings, discussion is almost always active and personalised: 'I think ...'; 'We did that last year...'; 'I don't think that's a good idea...'; 'I agree with John's suggestion....'; 'We need a new photocopier...'; 'Why can't we .....?'; 'What do people think about...?' and so on. People very rarely use the passive, past tense when speaking.

By writing minutes in the passive, past tense, the minutes are deliberately being rinsed of all emotion, personal involvement, active feelings and opinions. What emerges from the transformation from the active to the passive is the summary (or outcome) of the discussion, without reference or attribution to any individual. Although such writing is dull and boring to read, it is clear, objective and accurate.

Here are some further examples showing how active verbs can be replaced by the passive.

Active	Passive
I Jane informed the group that two additional volunteers were recruited during the open day.	I It was noted that two additional volunteers were recruited during the open day.
2 Mr Singh and Ms Brown thanked Jane for the extra work she had put in to make the open day such a success.	2 The co-ordinator was thanked for the extra work she had put in to make the open day such a success.
3 John Smith presented his report on progress towards the fundraising targets.	3 The manager's report on progress towards fundraising targets was noted.
4 Members asked whether the fundraising targets were achievable. Ahmed informed the group that there were still three months to go and that all the signs were looking good.	4 The group was informed that the fundraising targets were likely to be met within three months.
5 Njieri told the committee all about the positive progress on the outreach project.	5 It was noted that positive progress had been made on the outreach project.

6 The group discussed whether someone should attend the national conference to represent the region. Anna offered to go and the group agreed.	6 **Decision:** It was agreed that the region should be represented at the national conference by the co-ordinator. **Action:** Anna Smith.
7 The committee discussed the pros and cons of partitioning the waiting room to create a second interview room. Rita suggested getting some estimates for the building work. The committee asked for three different estimates in order to see whether there were sufficient funds in the budget. They decided to consider the matter again after estimates were received.	7 The proposal to partition the waiting room in order to create a second interview room was considered. **Decision:** A final decision on whether to proceed on the conversion was deferred pending receipt of three builders' estimates. **Action:** Rita Patel.
8 Paul mentioned the difficulties he was having with getting the necessary information about 2001's grant from the officers in Social Services. The group offered assistance but was not hopeful of things improving. Paul said he'd give them one more try.	8 The difficulty in obtaining information from Social Services about their grant aid for 2001 was noted. **Decision:** It was agreed that a further approach be made to Social Services to obtain information about their grant aid for 2001. **Action:** Paul Catchpole

You should not, however, feel that everything must be written in the passive and the past. If you find yourself getting tied in knots, the second rule comes into play: as well as being neutral, minutes must be clear and understandable.

For example, the following is not ideal:

> It was reported that the Director would be visiting the Basement Project which, it was thought, was a model project in the field of youth activities, and it was hoped that some committee members would be able to accompany her.

Several problems arise. Who thought the Basement Project was a good model? Was it a model in the past, or is it still a model? Who was hoping that committee members would go along – the Director or the committee? You could, without losing objectivity write:

> It was reported that the Director would be visiting the Basement Project, which in her opinion is a model project in the field of youth activities. She hoped that some committee members would be able to accompany her.

In the rewritten version, some of the verbs have been taken out altogether to avoid confusion ('in her opinion' instead of 'it was thought'), and some are in the active voice or present tense ('she hoped' and 'which ... is'). Note also that it has been broken into two separate sentences, as discussed later on.

Writing clearly, without losing precision

Advocates of 'plain English' argue that all writing, in order to be clear, should avoid language that is too formal or complex, even when it needs to be precise. There is no doubt that people find it easier to read and understand documents written in a more straightforward way.

When it comes to writing minutes, this is still true, even when you are depersonalising matters by using the passive voice. If your minutes do not need to be formal, you may also decide in the interests of clarity to use more active language. Be careful if you do this, however. Don't allow yourself to stray into a style that is imprecise or focused on individual views rather than collective decisions and actions.

The key points for writing plainer English are:

- As far as possible use words that people are familiar with. Don't use long words just because you think it sounds more 'official'.
- If you need to use jargon because it has a precise meaning, you must explain it unless you are sure that everyone reading the minutes will understand it.
- Try to write in short sentences. The general rule is 'one idea per sentence' (but you can break the rule if it doesn't work in a particular case).
- Keep your paragraphs reasonably short. You should start a new paragraph whenever there is a change of topic, or a change of approach.
- Use punctuation carefully; it can help people to understand what is going on.

You may find it helpful to ask someone to check your draft for clarity. If you have struggled to get the wording right in a particular place, they can tell you whether you've succeeded in making it clear. They will notice phrases that might be ambiguous, even though you knew exactly what you meant. And if you have left in sentences that are too convoluted, they can point them out.

Finding the right words for decisions

It is not good practice to mix and match phrases that indicate a decision. We strongly recommend that the same phrase be used throughout. Otherwise, people might start wondering whether the different words are supposed to reveal a different level of decision. If it was 'agreed', was that less enthusiastic than when it was 'resolved'? Any one of the following phrases is acceptable, provided that, having chosen one, you use it consistently:

> It was agreed to (or 'that') ...
>
> It was resolved that (or, just about, 'to') ...
>
> It was decided to (or 'that') ...

While you shouldn't mix the verbs (because then people might be looking for a difference in meaning that isn't really there), it is quite all right to use either 'to' or 'that', depending on the circumstances. 'To' is usually easier to use, especially when the subject of the next verb is the same as the one doing the agreeing. You might, for example, say:

> It was agreed to hold the AGM on 24 October.

The decision is being agreed by the management committee, and the management committee is equally responsible for holding the AGM. The alternative sounds, to many people, clumsier:

> It was agreed that the AGM should be held on 24 October.

When the action has to be done by someone else, however, you can't avoid 'that':

> It was agreed that Jenny Williams should represent the organisation at the next Council consultative meeting.

Minuting a vote

When you need to minute a vote, you must show how the vote came about. Here is an example:

The proposal to move all activities from the Community Centre to the Friends' Meeting House was discussed at length. Points in favour included:

(list of points)

Points against included:

(list of points)

A vote was then called for. The proposal was carried, with voting as follows:

In favour	4
Against	2
Abstentions	1

Decision: All activities of the society will take place at the Friends' Meeting House from now on, with the exception of those at the Community Centre which have already been confirmed and advertised.

Action: Secretary to inform the Community Centre, book rooms at the Meeting House and prepare a note to go out to all members at least two weeks before the first event at the Meeting House.

If the proposal is not carried, it is defeated.

Separating the decision from the action point

Usually a decision will have to be implemented by someone; someone has to put it into effect, and often within a specific time. This is known as the action point. The action point is not the same as the decision: it is always worth making the action separate, so as to draw sufficient attention to it. It is harder to follow up on whether people have done what they were supposed to do if the action point is locked into the text of the decision.

You should not write:

Decision: It was resolved that the Chair should write to the Council immediately to complain about the omission of cycling from their latest transport strategy.

The meeting may have made a decision, but it is far from clear to the chair, or anyone else reading the minutes, that this is in fact an action point. Far better to put:

Decision: It was agreed to write to the Council immediately to complain about the omission of cycling from their latest transport strategy.

Action: Chair.

This way, when the minutes come to be reviewed at the next meeting, everyone can immediately see that they should be expecting a report back to say, at least, that the letter was sent and, with luck, to give the response.

In informal minutes it may well be enough just to write 'Action:' and the name of the person doing it. Even in formal minutes, it may be completely obvious what the person has to do from the remainder of the minute. However, look back at the framework for minuting. You are not just interested in who, but also what and by when. Suppose you have a decision like this:

Decision: It was agreed that we should try to broaden our volunteer base by making a special effort to recruit volunteers from under-represented parts of the community, using new leaflets with a targeted distribution.

Action: William.

Here it is far from clear what William has to do or by when he is expected to have done it. The decision is much less likely to be implemented, because the minutes have given no way for it to be followed up. It is much better to put the details of the action in the 'Action:' part but to leave the principle in the 'Decision:' part:

Decision: It was agreed that we should try to broaden our volunteer base by making a special effort to recruit volunteers from under-represented parts of the community, using new leaflets.

Action: William Brown to produce a new leaflet within a month, aimed specifically at members of minority communities, and to produce a list for the next meeting of groups to approach as possible distribution points.

Of course, you cannot write a minute like this if the meeting didn't make such a clear decision. But if they did (possibly with your encouragement), then it is well worth separating the decision and the action in this way.

Here is another example where the decision, action and timescale have been combined:

Decision: It was agreed that Sharon would obtain at least three quotes from local hotels for booking a function room accommodating at least 70 people, catering and five bedrooms for the Annual General Meeting (AGM) in October 2002. It was also agreed that every effort be made to ensure that the quotations are available before the next meeting when a decision will need to be made on the dates, costs and venue for the AGM.

It would be much better to put:

Decision: It was agreed to obtain quotations from three local hotels for the costs of the Annual General Meeting due to be held in October 2002, to cover: a function room accommodating 70 people, catering and five bedrooms.

Action: Sharon Collier, Administrative Officer

Timescale: Quotations to be available for Management Committee meeting, due to be held on 11 November 2001.

In this example, unlike the previous ones, the timescale has been separated out again from the action. It is up to you whether you feel it is necessary; the minimum is to separate the decision and the action.

Finding the right words for other situations

When looking at the agenda, we established that there are five possible reasons for an item to be there. We have looked at how you might record the decisions and action points. It is worth considering items that are 'for information', 'for discussion', 'for approval' and 'for the record'.

'For information' items

The most useful word to the minute taker when minuting these items is 'noted'. This means that the meeting was aware of the information, but didn't take any decisions. There may have been an agenda item that said:

Report on Centenary appeal
To note that the appeal has now reached £14,000.

The minute would not even have to repeat what the agenda said. If the report was accepted without comment, it might just read:

Report on Centenary appeal

The report from the fundraiser was noted.

If people do comment or ask questions, the minutes can show this:

Report on Centenary appeal

The committee noted the report and congratulated the fundraising team.

or

Report on Centenary appeal

The report was noted. The appeal has now reached over 50% of its target.

'For discussion' items

Usually, items 'for discussion only' have a higher priority in meetings than items 'for information only'. This is because discussion items may ultimately lead to future decision making. Information can be shared and communicated by other means, but discussion can take place only at a meeting. The minute taker may have to judge whether to include the main points of the discussion or whether to rely on the standard sentence 'A full discussion took place'. You may find it useful to use phrases such as:

> During the discussion, the following points were made:

and then list them. Or, if there was a debate around a specific proposal, you might put:

> Points in favour of (or against) the proposal included:

and again list them. For advice on lists, see *Bullet points*, page 131.

'For approval' items

When minuting items for approval, it is usually unnecessary to record any of the discussion. Indeed, there shouldn't normally be much discussion, because the meeting is only reviewing decisions or actions that it has delegated to a specific person or another group.

There are four options with recommendations: they can be approved, approved with changes, rejected or deferred. Also, a meeting may be asked to ratify action that has already been taken.

Recommendations that are approved – these are easy to minute:

Working party recommendations on new membership structure (Background Paper 3)

Decision: The recommendations of the working party were approved.

Depending on what sort of recommendations you are considering, you may or may not have an action item. Rather than spelling out all the action from a complicated report, you should try to refer back to the recommendations themselves:

Action: Chief Executive to implement the recommendations and report back on progress to the next meeting.

Recommendations that are approved with changes – when minuting these, you must record what the changes are. If they are minor, the changes can be minuted as part of the decision:

Working party recommendations on new membership structure (Background Paper 3)

Decision: The recommendations of the working party were approved, with the amendment that the youth membership fee will be 40% of the full adult fee, not 50%.

If it is a major change, you are likely to have to minute more of the discussion and give the reasons for the change. If there are significant changes, it may be worth asking whether you can simply minute an indication of the key issues and send the working party, or one of its members, away to rewrite their recommendations.

Recommendations that are rejected – you will almost certainly need to minute the reasons for a recommendation being rejected. After the working party has put all that effort into their recommendations, they will not be happy just with a bald 'The recommendations of the working party were rejected'. This is one of the cases where you may well want to ask the meeting to clarify its reasons, so that the minutes can avoid giving unnecessary offence.

Recommendations that are deferred – if the meeting decides that it is not ready either to approve or reject the recommendations, then a decision is deferred. This is how your minute could read, showing any conditions that have to be met before the matter can be reconsidered:

Working party recommendations on new membership structure (Background Paper 3)

Decision: A decision on the recommendations of the working party was deferred, due to lack of time for a full discussion.

Action: Secretary to place this item on the next agenda.

Working party recommendations on new membership structure (Background Paper 3)

Decision: A decision on the recommendations of the working party was deferred.

Action: Working party to consider the impact of their proposals on the budget and to report back at the next meeting.

Action that needs ratifying – the final type of item for approval is where an action has already taken place but needs to be ratified. In this case, rejection is not really an option – even if the meeting doesn't like it, it's too late. Normally you will just minute their acquiescence:

Chair's emergency action on roof damage
The committee noted a report on the storm damage to the roof.
Decision: The Chair's action in authorising emergency repairs was ratified.

In the unlikely event that the meeting decides an action was unjustified, this is almost certain to be a major problem, because they will also have to consider how to deal with the disagreement. It may end up with the person resigning, or being demoted. You should probably seek the meeting's guidance on how it wants this minuted. A term you might find useful is 'censured' – which means not merely criticised, but criticised in a very formal way. You may also come across the term *ultra vires*, which means 'outside someone's powers'.

The Chair was censured for acting outside his authority (or 'for acting *ultra vires*').

Matters of this sort are often best recorded in a confidential minute (see *When and how to write a confidential minute*, page 135).

'For the record' items
Items for the record do not usually need to be 'noted'. They can simply be recorded as a fact. If you wanted to put apologies for absence as a separate minute (rather than as a heading at the start of the minutes alongside 'Present' and 'In attendance') you would write:

Apologies were received from …

not

It was noted that apologies had been sent by …

The approval and signing of previous minutes is also a matter of record. You would not put:

The minutes of the meeting held on 19 July 2001 were discussed.

Decision: The minutes were approved.

Instead you should just write:

> The minutes of the meeting held on 19 July 2001 were approved (or 'accepted as an accurate record') and signed.

If any corrections were made, you must note the full text of the corrections, exactly as they appear written by hand on the master copy, and indicate exactly where the correction should appear. Remember that people who have received only draft copies may want to update them with the correct wording. You would put something like:

> The minutes of the Finance Sub-committee meeting held on 3 February 2002 were approved as an accurate record, with the following correction – *insert text of correction* – and were signed by the Chair.

Where it says 'insert text of correction' you either have to explain it in narrative:

> The salary element of the new post is £24,000 excluding National Insurance (not including it).

> The new Accounts Manager is Paul Thompson (not Thomson).

or you have to say 'delete X and insert Y' or 'replace X with Y':

> Delete 'It was noted that the Council had gone back on its agreement to provide funds for three years' and insert 'The committee expressed its disappointment that the Council's original offer of three years' funding had now been reduced'.

> Insert 'for 2001/02' after 'the maximum liability'. (*This would mean that the correct minute should read 'the maximum liability for 2001/2002 … '.*)

> Replace 'travel would be reimbursed at 35p a mile' with 'travel would be reimbursed at the second class rail fare or, with prior approval, at 35p a mile for essential car use'.

If you find that you are writing a long correction, you may want to change the basic layout of the minute to look like this:

> The minutes of the Finance Sub-committee meeting held on 3 February 2002 were amended as follows:
>
> > Replace 'travel would be reimbursed at 35p a mile' with 'travel would be reimbursed at the second class rail fare or, with prior approval, at 35p a mile for essential car use.'

With this correction the minutes were approved as an accurate record and signed by the Chair.

Check your facts and figures

Because minutes are for the record, it is essential that they are accurate.

People are often sensitive about their names. Those with names that are hard to spell get used to weird and wonderful variations, but it doesn't mean they like it. It is a matter of common courtesy to get the name (and gender) right at all times. (The authors speak from personal experience of both these types of error.) If at all possible, you should check with the person themselves. Relying on someone else's idea of the correct spelling may just propagate a mistake rather than eliminating it.

Similarly with place names, it pays to get it right. While the mistake may be obvious if you write Walsall instead of Warsaw, it does nothing for people's confidence in the minutes. Check with the person who was talking, if necessary, to make sure that they really did mean Mottingham (in Greater London), not Nottingham, or that the area of Leicestershire pronounced 'Beaver' is actually spelled 'Belvoir'.

Figures can be the hardest of all. Try to encourage people who are presenting figures to put them on paper, preferably circulated beforehand. You may have to accept a paper tabled at the meeting. Failing that, encourage the person to put the figures up on a flip chart so that everyone at the meeting can see them. It will not only be the minute taker who loses track if they don't have the figures written down in front of them.

It is always advisable to check the figures you have minuted, either with the person involved or with a colleague, before the draft minutes are circulated. Once wrong information has been sent out, it tends to take on a life of its own. You would not want to be responsible if your draft minute showed a 5.2% pay rise, when it was actually 2.5%.

Finally, consider whether the actual figures need to be minuted at all. Obviously they will sometimes – as in the pay rise example – because the decision is actually about the figures. When the figures are just for background, however, the detail may not be necessary. For example:

> The meeting discussed the arrangements for the AGM. It was reported that the membership of the society had increased from 39 to 72 over the past year, which means that last year's venue would now be too small.

Decision: It was agreed to book the church hall for the AGM.
Action: Secretary.

Here, the important point is that the venue would be too small. The increase in membership is incidental. (It would be a different matter if the meeting were discussing membership and congratulating the membership secretary for getting so many new people to join.) You could avoid using the figures by saying:

The meeting noted that last year's AGM venue would be too small for the current number of members.
Decision: It was agreed to book the church hall for the AGM.
Action: Secretary.

Many people do not think numerically. If you are going to use numbers, you must explain what they mean. Unless there is a particular reason for being precise and going into detail, it will make much more sense for most people if you give just the rough headline figures, and refer them elsewhere for more detail. For example:

The final accounts for the year ended 30 June 2001 were received (see Finance Sub-committee minutes for details). The committee noted in particular that:

- A grant from the National Lottery meant that income was up by over £5,000.
- Staff costs still make up over three-quarters of expenditure.
- There was a small surplus on the year of about £2,200.

(Notice the 'in particular'. This is a way of pointing out that you have not necessarily included everything.)

Most style guides will suggest rules for when to write figures and when to spell out the numbers. The rules we favour are:

- Whole numbers up to ten should always be written out in full when they are part of the text.
- Numbers in times, dates and tables of figures may be written in figures, but always be consistent in your use of them.
- Percentages and numbers with a decimal part may be written in figures, but again, always be consistent.
- Numbers above ten may be written in figures, except at the start of a sentence.

These rules are all applied in the following examples:

The Chair announced that since three members were unable to arrive before 4.30 pm the meeting on 5 November 2001 had been retimed. (*But you would put 'four o'clock' or 'half past four', not '4 o'clock' or 'half past 4'.*)

It was reported that 103 membership renewals were outstanding. Twenty-seven of these were more than two months overdue. (*Or, 'Of these, 27 were more than two months overdue.'*)

The cost of living increase would average 3% for the year 2001/02. There are now seven permanent staff (5.4 full-time equivalents).

The numbers of branches in each region are:

North	7
South	13
East	8
West	5

With very large numbers, try not to confuse your readers. If possible, use the same units throughout. It would usually be better to put:

The total cost will be between £900,000 and £1,250,000.

instead of

The total cost will be between £900,000 and £1.25 million.

With millions, it is always better to write out 'million'. Instead of '£4m' you should write '£4 million'.

Write short sentences

Good minutes should be accurate, brief and clear (the ABC principle). Short sentences are always clearer than long ones.

Sentences get long for two reasons: when bits of ideas keep getting added on the end, and when two or more ideas are mixed up. The secret of writing shorter sentences is to recognise these two problems and apply the correct solution.

Watch out for words like 'and', 'although' and 'which'. They may (but don't always) mark a place where it is sensible to break a sentence into smaller, more digestible, chunks.

Take this example:

The meeting noted that there had recently been problems with parents who were collecting their children at the end of the session coming inside the building to wait and blocking the corridor, which was happening more and more as the weather got colder, and which was a safety hazard which we had already been warned about by the landlord.

The key point here is surely that there is a potential safety hazard, yet this idea is buried near the end of the sentence. The sentence itself is 59 words long; you should be aiming at something under 20 words in most of your sentences. By spotting the linking words it is possible to find suitable places to break the sentence up, while trying to get the ideas straight at the same time. The ideas are:

- There is a potential safety hazard.
- The hazard is caused by parents coming in and blocking the corridor.
- The landlords are concerned.
- The problem is getting worse.

This could lead to a rewritten minute as follows:

> The meeting noted a potential safety hazard. Parents waiting inside at the end of sessions are blocking the corridor. The landlords have already warned us about this. With the colder weather the problem is getting worse.

Not only does this version consist of four sentences instead of one; it is also only 37 words long.

Break up decisions and action points into shorter sentences as well. If someone is asked to do three different things, put them in three separate sentences. If a decision is made and the reason given, you may find it best to put the reason in a separate sentence, as in the following example:

Decision: It was decided not to order any large items of play equipment for the time being. Although there is enough money, there will be no storage space until the cupboard has had its new shelves fitted. It was also agreed that Sharon would take over responsibility for equipment ordering.

Action: Julie will:
- set aside £400 in the budget for large items of equipment
- chase the landlords over the next two weeks to find out when the cupboard shelves will be installed
- get the equipment catalogue sent to Sharon from now on.

It is important not just to write short sentences but to write complete ones. Otherwise, in your efforts to be brief you might become ambiguous. Look at this:

Date of Annual General Meeting
Deferred to 27 March 2002.

Does this mean the AGM has been deferred, or the discussion about it has been deferred? The minute should read either:

Date of Annual General Meeting
Discussion of this item was deferred to the meeting scheduled for 27 March 2002.

or

Date of Annual General Meeting
The Annual General Meeting has been deferred to 27 March 2002.

When to start a new paragraph

We have already recommended that you always use new paragraphs for decisions and for action items, as well as highlighting them with a clear heading. This draws people's attention to the most important parts of the minutes.

The most important time to start a new paragraph is when you introduce a new idea. If you are using the framework we have recommended (see page 96), each element in the framework should be in a separate paragraph. Your plan for a lengthy minute might therefore be:

Heading
Paragraph 1 – Setting the scene
Paragraph 2 – What happened next
Paragraph 3 – Points in favour of the proposal
Paragraph 4 – Points against the proposal
Paragraph 5 – Decisions
Paragraph 6 – Action points

and the resulting minute might read:

Proposal to close the Birmingham office (Background Paper 4)
The proposal to close the Birmingham office and transfer most of the posts there either to London or Leeds was discussed at length.

The views of the staff present were sought. Additional information on the running costs of the office was provided by the Treasurer. The committee noted that there is a legal requirement to consult the individuals affected before making redundancies.

Points in favour of the closure included:

- the overhead costs of running an additional office with relatively few staff;
- the changing balance of our work, which means that it is less important to have a presence in each region;
- the potential for new technology to allow staff to work from a distance.

Points against the closure included:

- the potential loss of high quality, experienced staff;
- the lack of a base in the Midlands for holding meetings;
- the effect it might have on members in the Midlands, giving the feeling that they were being abandoned.

Decision: It was decided, with regret, to close the Birmingham office. The cost of running the additional office was the main reason.

Action: Chief Officer to begin the process of consulting staff on the options of transfer or redundancy.

Chair, Chair of Finance Committee, Chief Officer and Deputy Chief Officer to prepare detailed plans for a smooth closure and transfer of workload.

Chair to write explanatory message for members, to appear prominently in the July newsletter (deadline 23 June).

If a whole minute can fit into two or three sentences, you may decide that you should just use one paragraph for everything except the decision and action points. Once it gets beyond that, think about breaking it up so that people can find the information they need easily.

Bullet points

When you are presenting a list of information, it is very easy for the reader to get lost. A good way to help them is to use bullet points. As well as being easier to read, these have the advantage that you can instantly see how many items there are in the list. If you need to refer to them later, it is easier to say 'third bullet point' than 'the sentence starting with "If" in the middle of the paragraph'. Also, when there is a lot to say, bullet points give you more options on punctuation.

Just to prove the point, the above paragraph could have been written:

When you are presenting a list of information, it is very easy for the reader to get lost. A good way to help them is to use bullet points. The advantages include:

- the information is easier to read;
- you can instantly see how many items there are in the list;
- if you need to refer to them later, it is easier to say 'third bullet point' than 'the sentence starting with "If" in the middle of the paragraph';
- when there is a lot to say, they give you more options on punctuation.

When using bullet points try to be consistent. Each bullet point should follow on in the same way from the introduction. The punctuation looks better if you use the same mark at the end of each bullet point, but always end with a full stop for the last point. Whole sentences tend to look better if they start with a capital letter and end with a full stop.

Here are some examples:

Decision: It was agreed to:
- review travel expenses limits;
- increase the overnight allowance to £45;
- apply the same rules to all staff across the board;
- introduce the new arrangements from 1 January 2003.

The criteria on which the entries will be judged are:
- creativity
- replicability
- value for money.

PART FIVE

Questions and specific situations

16 When and how to write a confidential minute

Minutes are often a public document. Some people may have the right to see them, or they may be widely distributed as a means of sharing information (although this is not usually to be recommended).

However, meetings often discuss matters that are confidential, either because they relate to specific individuals or because they need to be kept secret for a while. In this case, you need to write a confidential minute.

This need should be identified during the meeting. The chair may say 'Please make this a confidential minute', or you may ask whether it should be a confidential minute if you feel it appropriate. It could be, however, that you only realise after the meeting that an item might qualify for a confidential minute. In this case the best option is to ask the chair of the meeting for guidance. If this is not possible, and no one else can advise you, err on the side of caution. If you write a confidential minute and it turns out not to be necessary, you can always circulate it; but if you circulate something that should have been kept confidential, there is no way to get the information back when you find out.

A confidential minute is written in a separate place from the other minutes. Apart from that, there is no difference in the way you write it. The main minutes *must* indicate that the confidential minute exists, without breaking confidentiality. So you might write:

3a. Fundraiser's salary
See confidential minute book.

or:

7. Bid for Council advice contract
The Committee discussed at length whether to put in a bid for the Council contract.

Decision: It was agreed that it would be appropriate to make a bid (for details, see confidential minutes book).

In the first example, it was not appropriate even to disclose the issue in detail. In the second, the fact of the bid would not be a secret, but the details – such as how much the bid was for and how it would be delivered – would be confidential until after the decision had been made, and perhaps even beyond.

Where to record confidential minutes

Confidential minutes must, of course, be kept separate from the regular minutes if their confidentiality is to be preserved. If you frequently write confidential minutes, ensure that they are kept in a separate book (or ring binder), similar to the main one and labelled in the same way.

For the very occasional confidential minute, it may not be worth having a book. However, you then have to think about how you will keep the record safely. One idea might be to seal the minute in an envelope after it has been approved, labelling the outside with the title and date of the meeting. The sealed envelope could be kept with the regular minutes.

Some organisations keep their confidential minute book in the safe, rather than in open filing cabinets alongside other material.

Each confidential minute must identify precisely the meeting it relates to and the number of the minute in the regular minutes. The minute would be something like this:

Management Committee meeting held on 23 April 2000 (Meeting I of 00/01)

Agenda item 3a: Fundraiser's salary
A request was received from the Fundraiser for a performance-related salary increase.

Decision: The Committee acknowledged the recent fundraising successes, but decided that it would not be appropriate to award an increase because:

- The Committee has previously decided against performance-related pay on principle.

- There is no equivalent provision in the Fundraiser's salary for a reduction in the case of future poor performance.

- No other staff would have the opportunity to benefit, even though many had contributed to the fundraising.

Action: Chair and General Manager to propose alternative ways of recognising this good performance, for approval at the next Personnel Committee meeting.

Confidential minutes must also be approved and signed

Decisions recorded in confidential minutes are as much a part of the business of a meeting as any other decisions. The minutes must therefore be approved and signed in just the same way. However, it may not be appropriate to circulate the minute in advance. In this case, it would be necessary to read the minute out at the meeting where it was to be approved.

17 Uses and abuses of action sheets

An action sheet is a list of tasks arising from a meeting. In the best of all possible worlds, we might assume that people present at a meeting would make their own notes to remind themselves of the tasks they have been allocated. Sadly, this is not often the case.

If there is a delay of more than a few days in the production and circulation of draft minutes, tasks may be overlooked or forgotten. In some cases, the deadline for undertaking a particular task may have passed before the draft minutes are circulated. To help overcome these problems, some organisations use action sheets, circulated straight away, in advance of the minutes.

Other organisations use action sheets accompanying the minutes to pull together all the agreed action items into a handy reference format. In this case the action sheet will be circulated alongside the draft minutes.

Some organisations do not use action sheets at all, relying instead on the minutes to remind people about their tasks.

If you are going to use action sheets in connection with a formal meeting, we recommend that:

1   Before writing up the minutes the minute taker should go through the notes from the meeting and extract all the decisions and action points that were agreed.

2   These should be typed up and circulated to the people to whom the tasks have been allocated.

3   Each recipient's name should be highlighted so that their attention is drawn immediately to the task they are supposed to undertake.

4   Because the minutes are awaiting approval, the status of decisions and tasks remains 'unconfirmed' or 'draft'. For this reason, the action sheet should remind people that they may need to obtain appropriate authorisation before undertaking their tasks.

Here is a sample layout of an action sheet.

Draft Action Sheet

Newtown Women's Refuge
Personnel Sub-Committee (PSC) Meeting, held on 5 March 2002
As the minutes of this meeting have not yet been approved, please obtain any necessary authorisations before implementing these decisions.

Decisions	Action	By when
Recruit p/time play worker to vacant post Advertise locally in press, job centres etc. Use existing job description, pay-scale, person spec. Plan shortlisting schedule and interview date	Deputy Manager, Sue Baines	As soon as possible
Revise induction and probation programme to incorporate new health & safety policy	Manager, Donna James	By end May
Consult staff on the introduction of flexi-time working hours. Report findings to PSC.	Sue Baines	By end April

If the meeting is formally constituted, the production of a separate action sheet is not a substitute for the minutes. The action sheet is produced in addition to the minutes. The minutes themselves must still contain the full text of all the decisions, and the action points.

Action sheets and informal meetings

Some informal meetings may not need detailed minutes at all. *Ad hoc* groupings, or informal task groups working on particular projects within a limited time period, can rely on action sheets alone, rather than minutes. This saves time and resources and is very much more effective than waiting for the production of minutes. The action sheet should be written up by hand *during* the meeting, and copied and circulated to all concerned immediately. (If you wish, the hand-written version can be typed up for clarity.) There should be no need for a dedicated minute taker at such meetings. Instead, one person should be nominated by the group to write up and circulate the actions.

Here is an example:

Golf Tournament Planning Group Meeting 15 June 2002

Action agreed	Who	By when
Commission design of flyers and leaflets	Narinder	end June
Get estimates for printing of tickets	James	end June
Recruit 10 volunteer stewards	James	end July
Prepare draft press releases	Colin	end July
Book disco for party	Colin	asap
Confirm date in writing with golf club	James	immediately
When the date is confirmed in writing, send letter to all members. Enclose a form asking them to indicate their interest and whether they can help with circulation of flyers etc.	Carol	end June

18 Minuting an annual general meeting

There are few meetings in a voluntary organisation more formal than its AGM. If the organisation is a company limited by guarantee, much of this formality is required by the Companies Act, if not by the organisation's own memorandum and articles of association.

Occasionally, other meetings will be run on the same formal rules. So that you are not stumped by being asked to minute them, we give an outline of the procedures here. What we are not able to do is to give the whole story about how formal meetings are run. The chair should either consult written standing orders, or ask the organisation to set up a standing orders committee to give advice and guidance.

At an AGM (or any other general meeting) you should not minute any of the discussion. All the reasons we have previously discussed apply, plus the fact that the minutes will probably not be circulated until nearly a year later. By the time they come out, no one's memory of what went on will be reliable. If your organisation wants a detailed record of the discussion, it must be clear that this is a separate exercise from producing the minutes. Often, in any case, the proposer(s) of a resolution will build into it a justification for the decision they are seeking, or will provide a background paper setting out their arguments.

If you have a speaker as part of the event surrounding the AGM, this will not normally be part of the formal business and therefore doesn't need to be minuted. If, however, the organisation wants a record of this, you can just state the fact of the presentation:

I. Guest speaker

The Secretary of State for the Voluntary Sector made a presentation, and was warmly thanked by the Chair.

Of course, if there is a printed version of the speech, you can circulate this with the minutes, but not as part of the minutes.

What you have to do is ensure that the minutes demonstrate that the meeting was properly run. This may mean recording elections, and it also means understanding the more formal way of making decisions by resolution.

Tellers

A formal meeting will often have tellers to count the votes and announce the result to the chair. What you have to minute is the outcome. Since the tellers will have written down the result, you should get the exact figures from them, after the meeting if necessary. You should minute the appointment of tellers, so that people can judge their independence for themselves:

> **2. Appointment of tellers**
> John Brown and Victoria Saxe-Coburgh were appointed as tellers for the meeting.

Once this has been done, the tellers determine the outcome of any ballot or show of hands.

Elections

For elections, you must record how the decision was made and the outcome. You do not have to list the details of the candidates and their proposers and seconders, because these will already be either on the agenda or on separate ballot papers. For example:

> **3. Election of trustees**
> A secret ballot was held for the two trustee vacancies. The voting, including postal votes, was as follows:
>
> | | |
> |---|---|
> | William McGonagle | 23 |
> | Edward Lear | 17 |
> | Alfred Tennyson | 15 |
> | Lewis Carroll | 5 |
>
> William McGonagle and Edward Lear were therefore elected as trustees to serve until November 2004.

When there is only one candidate, you still have to record this:

> Hildegard of Bingen was elected unopposed for a fifth term as chair.

Resolutions

Resolutions must be proposed and, if your governing document says so, seconded. The names of the proposer and seconder should appear on the agenda. Sometimes, a branch or other organisational member can propose resolutions as well as, or instead of, individuals. Resolutions must be written down and, except in a genuine emergency, circulated in advance on the agenda. A resolution spells out exactly the decision that is being asked for:

Resolution 3. Membership criteria

From 1 April 2002 full membership of the society will be open to those aged between 16 and 18 who have been active junior members for at least two years.

Proposed: Nell Gwynn
Seconded: Emma Hamilton

Your minute should start by repeating the resolution number, title, text, proposer and seconder, exactly as it appears on the agenda. You then record the decision, in whatever way it happened:

After debate, the resolution was carried on a show of hands.

or

After a full debate, a poll was called for. The voting was 18 in favour, 23 against. The resolution was therefore defeated.

It is not necessary to record abstentions in a general meeting, unless you feel the need to show that a quorum was present for the vote.

If the chair exercises a casting vote, you should record this:

The voting was tied 19 in favour, 19 against.

The Chair exercised her casting voting against the resolution, which was therefore defeated.

Amendments

Life gets more complicated when your organisation's standing orders allow for amendments to be put to resolutions, especially if these can be put forward during the meeting as well as in advance. The rule still applies that amendments must be in writing, and again they need a proposer and possibly a seconder (see your governing document). For the minutes, it is important that you get the exact wording of the amendment, either from the agenda or – if the amendment is put at the meeting – from the proposer (or the chair, if they have asked to be given the text).

An amendment aims to change the resolution (but is not allowed to reverse its intention completely). Some organisations allow amendments to be proposed to amendments. This is usually a recipe for total confusion, but we have covered this possibility in the discussion below, so that you know what to do if it happens. The order in which you minute events (which should match the order in which they happen), is this:

1   Quote the substantive resolution from the agenda (as above under *Resolutions*).

2   Then quote the first amendment to be discussed. Take careful note if the chair and/or the standing orders committee decides to take amendments in a different order from that on the agenda.

3   Give the decision on the first amendment.

4   Go on in the same way with the second, third and subsequent amendments.

5   If there is an amendment to an amendment, quote the main amendment, then deal with its amendment, then finish with the outcome on the main amendment.

6   Once you have covered all the amendments, quote the revised resolution if any changes have been made.

7   Give the decision on the substantive resolution.

To illustrate this, we take the example we have used above, but assume now that two amendments have been proposed in advance. On one of these amendments a further amendment is proposed during the meeting. Your minute might look like this:

Resolution 3. Membership criteria
From 1 April 2002 full membership of the society will be open to those aged between 16 and 18 who have been active junior members for at least two years.

Proposed: Nell Gwynn   Seconded: Emma Hamilton

Amendment 3a.
Replace 'two years' with 'one year'.

Proposed: Quorn branch

After debate, this amendment was carried on a show of hands.

Amendment 3b.
Add to resolution 'subject to approval by the executive committee'.

Proposed: Wat Tyler   Seconded: Lambert Simnel

During the debate, the following amendment was proposed by the Quorn branch:

> Replace 'executive committee' with 'branch to which they belong'.

This amendment was defeated by acclamation.

After debate, amendment 3b was carried on a show of hands.

Amended Resolution 3.

The following resolution, as amended, was then debated and put to a vote:

> From 1 April 2002 full membership of the society will be open to those aged between 16 and 18 who have been active junior members for at least one year, subject to approval by the executive committee.

Votes were cast as follows:

> For: 27   Against: 6

The amended resolution was therefore carried.

Sometimes the proposer of a resolution will realise that an amendment improves the original. Standing orders may allow the proposer to accept the change without any discussion by the meeting. If they do this, you must minute the fact. Following on from the discussion above, we will assume a third amendment. Your minute might then read:

Amendment 3c

Delete '1 April 2002' and insert '1 January 2002'.

> Proposer: executive committee

This amendment was accepted by the proposer of the resolution.

Amended Resolution 3.

The following amended resolution was then debated and put to a vote:

From 1 January 2002 full membership of the society will be open to those aged between 16 and 18 who have been active junior members for at least one year, subject to approval by the executive committee.

Votes were cast as follows:

> For: 27   Against: 6

The amended resolution was therefore carried.

Points of order and other interruptions

A 'point of order' is a device used to interrupt proceedings with the claim that the business of the meeting is not being properly conducted. The standing orders will normally say that the chair must immediately consider the point of order and decide whether it is valid, with the help of the standing orders committee if there is one. There is no need to minute points of order. They are an interruption to the business of the meeting, not part of it. Your minuting should resume once the business is resumed. If the outcome changes the course of the meeting, however, you may need to minute this:

> On a point of order, the chair ruled that amendment 2b should not be put to the meeting, since it sought to negate the resolution entirely.

If someone proposes a procedural resolution, you should minute it in the same way as any other resolution. For instance, during a discussion someone may propose that the resolution 'be now put'. In other words they want to cut short the discussion and go straight to a decision. If the standing orders allow this, the chair may make a ruling or ask the meeting to decide. Either way you should minute it. For example:

> During the debate, Asha Patel proposed that the resolution be now put. This was defeated on a show of hands and the debate continued.

Attendance

If you have an accurate attendance record you may list all the names of those present in the minutes of an AGM, but you don't have to. It is normally enough to indicate how many members were present (to demonstrate that there was a quorum). Another common practice is to list the key people – such as the committee and guests – and then to put something like 'and 26 members', or even 'and about 20 members', if people tended to come and go during the meeting.

19 Minuting meetings that take decisions about individuals

A variety of issues come into play if you are asked to minute meetings that are taking decisions about individuals, such as:

- case conferences
- discipline hearings, grievances and complaints
- grant-making or award-making panels
- appointment panels.

The outcome of such a meeting will generally be a clear decision – to take specific action, to issue a warning or not, to give a grant or not or to select a particular applicant. If the decision concerns a sensitive or personal matter, the chair may decide that the minutes should include the reason for the decision. It may also be necessary to show, through the minutes, that all the relevant information was taken into account in reaching the decision. For example the minutes may need to show that an individual got a fair hearing and that their views were adequately represented.

Ideally, the chair should sum up these matters and confirm them with the meeting for the record. If the chair does not summarise, the minute taker should propose a form of words to the meeting for their approval. It is essential that the reasons be those of the meeting, not the assumptions of the minute taker.

Whenever a judgement is being made, there will almost inevitably be a subjective element, but the reason given should be as precise and factual as possible. It is not so important to give reasons for a positive decision, although the meeting may want a comment to be recorded.

For each of the four types of meeting, specific issues may arise.

Case conferences

Case conferences concern individuals who may be vulnerable or at risk. They may be children, adults with learning difficulties or people with mental illness. Case conferences may involve the staff of just one organisation, or they may bring together people from several public and voluntary sector agencies to consider the most appropriate course of action. The individual or their family may or may not be present.

Minuting case conferences is a highly skilled activity. The matters discussed may be strictly confidential to those present. In some case conferences it may be necessary to minute the views of each agency involved: in others, it may not. The wording of the decision and action points should be checked at the time, with those present. The decision may be conveyed to the particular individual, or their family, immediately after the case conference, so it is vital that the members of the case conference have an opportunity to check the text of the decision before it is acted upon.

The points to bear in mind when minuting case conferences are:

- to check, at the outset, what type of minutes are required and especially whether all aspects of the process should be minuted, or whether the minutes should be confined to the decision and action points;
- to document any concerns on which no action is to be taken but over which a watch is to be kept;
- to clarify whether you should write down only that information which can be shared with the client.

Discipline hearings, grievances and complaints

For hearings which are part of a process in which the two sides are hoping to have a continuing relationship, the most important point about the written record is usually that either it should be agreed by both sides or it should, at least, clearly identify any disagreements. It is therefore common to produce a draft statement of the outcome that will form the written record of the hearing once it has been agreed. This is not strictly a minute, since it will often sum up the opposing positions as well as the outcome, and will need to identify who said what.

If the two sides make written submissions, there is no need to repeat these in the record. If the hearing is based on verbal submissions, these must be summed up, in as neutral and dispassionate a way as possible.

Grant-making panels

Where a panel is making grants or awards to a number of people or groups in one session, detailed minutes are not normally required. What is essential to record is:

- the exact amount of money or other benefit agreed;
- any conditions that have to be met before the award can be released;
- any phasing of the award – for example some may be paid immediately, but further instalments will follow only after certain events have taken place.

It may also be the panel's policy to record:

- any reasons for rejecting an application, or reducing the amount;
- any favourable comments the panel makes, either on approved or rejected applications.

It is usually more important to record reasons for rejecting or reducing an award than for agreeing it. Applicants may need to be told why they have not succeeded. In such a case the reason must be that of the panel collectively, and the chair should summarise the reason for the benefit of both the minute taker and panel members.

Appointment panels

It is essential that *all* the paperwork and panel members' notes are kept for at least three months after an appointment is made. If one of the unsuccessful candidates makes a claim for discriminatory treatment they will be entitled to call for all the papers to be made available to the employment tribunal.

For this reason, formal minutes are less important. It is unusual to have a separate minute taker, and there is no need for additional detailed notes. However, there is still some value in preparing a clear summary of the outcome of the discussion, as in this example:

Appointment panel for finance clerk, 24 October 2001

Panel: XX (Finance Director), XX (Treasurer), XX (Personnel Officer)

Candidates' aggregate scores (each panel member scoring out of five) against the person specification:

Candidate:	A	B	C	D
Previous experience	12	13	9	8
Qualifications	10	12	7	12
Written exercise	14	9	10	6
Understanding of current finance issues	11	10	10	8
Communication skills	9	11	8	6

Decision: to appoint Candidate A, subject to references. In the case of references being unsatisfactory or Candidate A turning the job down, it will be offered to Candidate B, again subject to references.

Reasons for rejection:

Candidate B – significantly less good than Candidate A on the written exercise, which represents the major part of the job, although good in all other areas.

Candidate C – underqualified and less experienced compared with other candidates.

Candidate D – well qualified but less good on all other criteria.

Whoever has to write to the candidates with the outcome can use the written decisions as the basis for any feedback they give the candidates.

20 Minuting meetings without agendas

Remember that there is no secret or unwritten law which states that when there are three or more people gathered in a room to discuss something, then a fourth person must be brought in to minute their meeting.

Informal meetings

There are situations where meetings are arranged without agendas. In some cases, the start of the meeting will be devoted to agreeing an agenda. In other cases, there may be no need to do this, as there is only one matter to be discussed. There are a number of ways of dealing with this, which are set out below.

The meeting should, first of all, make a decision as to whether minutes are necessary. The decision will rest on the importance of the meeting. Traditional minutes may not be appropriate for informal meetings, get-togethers, working groups, consultative open meetings and the like. If other people, not present at the meeting, need to know the meeting's outcome, an informal note, report, bulletin or announcement will suffice. The text of this can be agreed at the end of the meeting, and issued as soon as possible after the meeting. When conveying information in this way, it is not necessary to use the formal language of minutes.

On page 152 is an example of a short, informative report of a meeting's outcome. If there is no reason to report the proceedings to others, then there is no need for minutes or a report of the meeting.

Note to all volunteer representatives. Please pass on to all volunteers.

Meeting of volunteer representatives, held at Head Office on 1 March 2001

The volunteer co-ordinator, Jane Briggs, held a special meeting of the volunteer representatives today. They had identified a number of issues arising from volunteers' experiences of home visiting, and these were discussed in a very constructive way. There was a lot of discussion about personal safety, and particularly about the use of volunteers' own mobile phones. Jane will be reporting the main points of the discussion to the next management team meeting on March 20th and will let us know their response straight away. If you want further information, please contact Jane Briggs or Sally Martin.

Sally Martin, Volunteer representative. 1 March 2001

Think-tank, single issue meetings to share ideas

Many voluntary organisations arrange meetings to pool ideas about particular issues or problems. The purpose of such meetings is to gather in everyone's thoughts in order to arrive at possible solutions or to make progress on a special issue. In these situations, although it may be important to record the ideas that emerge, it may not be appropriate or necessary to produce traditional minutes. The convenor of the meeting should consider at the outset whether and how the meeting will be written up. The record of such a meeting can be produced in any number of ways. Here are three suggestions.

A simple summary of the ideas which emerged

This would be written in plain English, using a conversational tone, rather than formal minute-writing language. For example:

Lots of good ideas emerged at today's meeting of the fundraising team, which was called to discuss the recent 10% shortfall in our targets. The team now feels a lot more positive about the future than it did last week, when the figures came in.

Suggestions that were favoured by the team were:

1. To arrange a celebrity golf tournament.

2. To ask the local college whether they would adopt us for their rag week.

3. To promote more payroll giving.

4. To recruit more volunteers to build up our community fundraising.

If anyone else is sitting on some good ideas, please let us know. We'll be finalising our plans at the next meeting on 8 June, and would welcome your ideas before then.

John Martin – Fundraising Co-ordinator.

A brief report

This would set out the result or outcome of the discussions. For example:

The fundraising team met today to discuss our fundraising strategy, following the disappointing shortfall in our fundraising targets. More work will need to be done before a strategy is finalised at our next meeting on 8 June. If you want to know more or have any ideas, contact John Martin, Fundraising Co-ordinator.

A simple announcement

This could be as follows:

The fundraising team is working on some good ideas for our strategy. We'll be developing them in the next couple of weeks and will let you all know the final outcome after our next meeting on June 8th.

It should not be necessary to appoint a minute taker at such meetings. Instead, participants should be encouraged to take their own notes, or to write up their ideas on a flip chart. The notes on the flip chart can then be converted into any one of the above examples.

Appendix A

Sample minutes

Minutes of the Oldtown Community Centre Management Committee, held at the Oldtown Community Centre, 340 High Street, Oldtown, Leicester on Wednesday 24 October 2001

Present
Lady Jane Grey (in the Chair)
Lee Comer
Josiah Equiano
Gill Taylor (Treasurer) (until 4.30pm, not present for minutes 7 to 11)
Paul Ticher

In attendance
Mary Seacole (Centre Manager)
Harold Godwinson (Caretaker)
PC Dixon (Community Liaison Officer)
Darth Vader (Oldtown Social Services)

Apologies for absence
Robert Scott

The meeting started at 3.00pm

1.   Welcome and introductions
The Chair welcomed everyone to the meeting and introduced PC Dixon, our new community liaison officer.

2.   Presentation from PC Dixon
PC Dixon spoke to the meeting about his role, and distributed leaflets explaining how to contact him (copy attached). He was thanked by the Chair on behalf of the meeting.

3. **Minutes of the previous meeting**
    The minutes of the meeting held on 19 July were approved as an accurate record with one correction – Josiah Equiano's name was mis-spelled – and were signed by the Chair.

4. **Proposal to cut council grant**
    The meeting discussed information from the Centre Manager that rumours of a possible cut to the grant next year appeared to be true.

    In a detailed discussion, the meeting satisfied itself that this was a serious possibility and considered the likely effects on many other local voluntary organisations if the centre's funding was reduced.

    Members expressed their disappointment that this was not the first time the council had appeared to change its funding decisions without consultation and at short notice.

    Decision: It was agreed to lobby the council over the proposed cut to the grant. The main basis of our argument would be that having just paid for the extension to our building, it would be inconsistent for the council to deny us the funds to operate it.

    Action: Mary Seacole to write a letter to the local councillors and our grants officer, by 29 October, and to try to arrange a follow-up meeting with them.

5. **Financial report (see background paper)**
    [Members asked for this item to be taken earlier than it appeared on the agenda, because of its impact on the following item.]

    The Treasurer's report was received and noted. Concern was expressed that the projected income figure for the Christmas fête might be optimistic. The Treasurer explained that this includes a substantial amount from sponsorship and advertising in the programme, which is already confirmed.

    The committee congratulated all concerned on an excellent start to the financial year.

---

6.   Staffing

6a.   Proposed office manager post

The proposal to create a post of part-time office manager was discussed in detail.

Decision: The post will be created as quickly as possible. Pending the job evaluation, the salary will be on the same scale as the Outreach Worker.

Action: Centre Manager to report back on progress at next meeting.

6b.   Caretaker's salary

[Harold Godwinson was asked to leave the room during this item.] See confidential minute book.

[At this point Gill Taylor left the meeting.]

7.   Report on refurbishment of toilets

The completion of work to refurbish the toilets was noted. Discussion ensued on further areas of work that will be required within the next five years.

Action: Caretaker to present costed proposals on future refurbishment to the next meeting.

8.   Chair's emergency action on roof damage

The committee noted a report on the storm damage to the roof.

Decision: The Chair's action in authorising emergency repairs was ratified.

9.   Users' newsletter

A discussion took place on whether the users' newsletter should be redesigned.

Decision: It was agreed that research be undertaken to establish whether there is a need for a redesign and what the associated costs would be.

Action: Centre Manager to ask Outreach Worker for a report to the next meeting.

OLDTOWN COMMUNITY CENTRE MANAGEMENT COMMITTEE, 24.10.01, PAGE 3 OF 4   *J. G.* (CHAIR)

10. Other matters arising from previous minutes

10a. Complaint over unwashed coffee cups

The Centre Manager reported that this problem now appeared to have been resolved, through talks with both parties.

10b. Twin town visit

The visitors from Plomeur Bodou in Brittany spent half an hour touring the centre and meeting representatives of various voluntary organisations. (See reports in the local press and our newsletter.)

11. Any other business

11a. Booking clash

The Chair had been approached by both the Brownies and the Women's Institute over a booking clash on Saturday 13 October. On investigation, this appeared to be due to human error in agreeing a change but not recording it accurately.

Decision: It was agreed to apologise to all concerned and to remind staff to use the correct procedure for making **and changing** bookings.

Action: Chair to write letters of apology.
Centre Manager to remind staff.

11b. Christmas lights

The Chair informed the meeting that the Christmas lights would be switched on at 6.00pm on Saturday 24 November, and all were welcome to attend.

The meeting finished at 5.15pm.

Date of next meeting

Tuesday 15 January 2002, at the Community Centre, beginning at 3.00pm.

Signed: .... *Jane Grey* (CHAIR) ....

Date: .... 15.1.02 ....

Appendix B

Sample abbreviations for use in note taking

W 8 C	wait and see – in due course – in the near future
B4	before – in advance
L8r	later – afterwards
1/7 ... 3/7	I week ... 3 weeks
1/24 ... 3/24	I day ... 3 days
3/12 ... 5/12	3 months ... 5 months
afdtp	a full discussion took place
iwa	it was agreed
=	equal opportunities
cwe	concern was expressed (or ⬇ or ☹)
ⓘ	very important – everyone to take note
>>	greater – more – increase
<<	less than – decrease – reduce
⇧	pass upwards – refer to a higher authority
◀	distribute or circulate widely
Σ	calculate – work out what it will cost
#	not very good – could have been improved (hash sign)
≅	further research – find out more
©	strictly confidential
☂	will depend on the weather
🚗	transport to be arranged
⌷	start new file/project/activity
M̄	the matter was deferred to a later date
ŵ	together with
pma	previous minutes approved
↻	will have to try again – repeat this activity
↑	will depend on what happens
~	await reply

ℙ	team to take responsibility
∞	at some point in the future
ℰ	need to consult widely on this
ℂ	make contact with
U̲	very urgent
®	report back
donm	date of next meeting
↔	extend – widen – lengthen
@	action point or A
PU	passed unanimously
fpm	the following points were made

Glossary

Acclamation By voice, when a decision is made. People call out 'aye' or 'nay' (or 'yes' or 'no'). The decision is made by acclamation.

Agenda The plan for a meeting, usually sent out in advance, and showing what is to be discussed.

AGM Annual general meeting: the general meeting that most organisations must hold once a year to consider certain routine business – and other business if there is any.

AOB Any other business: an item on the agenda that allows people to raise emergency issues or small information points which they did not put on the agenda in advance. Not to be used as an excuse to avoid preparing major agenda items in advance and giving proper notice.

Apologies Short for 'apologies for absence'. Advance notice from someone who is expected to be at a meeting, or who has been invited, saying that they will not be able to attend.

Approve Used formally when recommendations are made to a meeting and they are accepted, especially with little or no amendment.

Attendance Those who are at a meeting but do not have a vote are 'in attendance'. It is normal to explain in the minutes why they are there.

Authorise To allow someone to do a specific thing, but with less leeway for making their own decisions than if the matter is delegated.

Ballot A vote made by each person writing their choice on separate pieces of paper, which are then counted. A secret ballot means that the papers must be unidentifiable, and must be put secretly into a box or other receptacle then taken out and counted.

Business The activities of a meeting that lead (or may lead) to decisions.

Calling notice Information about where and when a meeting will take place, which must be sent in good time to all those entitled to attend the meeting. Often incorporated into the agenda or sent with it.

Company secretary A role in a company, with specific duties set out by law. Only a full-time job in very large companies, so usually a role held by the chief officer or finance director. The company secretary should attend board meetings, and it is not unknown for them to take the minutes.

Consensus General agreement. Strictly a consensus is when everyone agrees; in practice it can be used when those who disagree are content to go along with the majority.

Co-opted Brought onto a committee by the other members of the committee, as opposed to being elected by a wider body, appointed by another organisation, or being there ex officio.

Correspondence received A common agenda item for organisations which do not have registered offices and paid staff. The organisation's address will often be a member's home address, to which all correspondence is sent. In such cases, the organisation's meetings may be the only opportunity to review the correspondence. The minute taker records those items of correspondence which were considered at the meeting.

Defer To leave the decision on a matter until a future meeting, either because there is no time, or the meeting becomes inquorate or there is some piece of information which is lacking.

Delegate To give someone a job to do, with full powers to take action or make a decision. If a task has been delegated to a person or group they have to report back on what they have decided or done, but do not have to get the main meeting's approval. Do not use 'delegated' if a person or group has been asked to look into something or get information which the main group or committee will then make a decision on. There are usually some tasks that a meeting is not allowed to delegate.

Ex officio Because of their job. Someone may have the right to attend a meeting ex officio.

General meeting A meeting of all the members of a company or association. Most organisations have at least one routine general meeting a year – the 'Annual' General Meeting – with any other general meetings called 'Special' or 'Extraordinary' General Meetings.

Governing document The document (or documents) that set out how an organisation is to be run. A company limited by guarantee will have two documents, a short memorandum of association and longer articles of association that contain more detailed rules. These are usually referred to together as the memorandum and articles or 'mem & arts'. Other organisations may have a constitution or a trust deed.

Inquorate The situation a meeting is in when a quorum is not present.

Interests Connections, usually financial, which might be thought to influence someone's decision. For example, a committee member who owns (or whose family owns) a company that is tendering for a contract has an 'interest'. Depending on the meeting and its terms of reference, people may have to declare any interests before participating in the discussion or decision; they may have to withdraw from the meeting; or they may be barred from membership if they have relevant interests. If someone declares an interest this must be minuted.

Matters arising An item on the agenda which provides the meeting with an opportunity to be kept informed of developments which have taken place relating to decisions made or matters discussed at the previous meeting. It is usually placed near the top of the agenda, but it can just as easily be placed near the end. Items for discussion should not be put under matters arising, but should be given their own slot on the agenda, even if they relate back to a previous minute.

Minute book The bound book or ring binder holding the agreed, signed minutes. Must be clearly labelled and kept in a safe place, as it is an important document. Must be available for consultation by all those entitled to see the minutes.

Minute-taking notebook A book reserved for taking the notes of a series of meetings. Should be kept safe by the minute taker. Does not normally have to be available to anyone else, but others should know where to find it if necessary.

Nem. Con. *Nemine contradicente* – with no one disagreeing.

Notes What the minute taker writes during the meeting if they are going to write the minutes afterwards. If the minute taker is writing directly into the minute book or file by hand, and if they are approved and signed at that meeting, these are minutes, not notes.

Poll A counted vote, either by ballot or show of hands.

Present Attending a meeting as a member – i.e. with a vote.

Proposer The first person who puts their name to a resolution. They must be entitled to do so (for example by being a member of the organisation).

Proxy Someone who acts at a meeting on behalf of someone else. It is not unusual for someone to be in the position of casting their own vote as well as one or more proxy votes. Each vote counts in the decision; however, the proxy votes do not usually count towards the quorum – which is based on the number of people present.

Quorate The situation the meeting is in when a quorum is present.

Quorum The minimum number of people *with a vote*, who need to be present in order for a meeting to be valid, and therefore for its decisions to count.

Ratify To say that a decision or action which was made by someone, or a group, on behalf of the meeting was acceptable. Normally such action is taken in an emergency, and it is often too late to change it. Ratification is therefore usually a formality. Nevertheless it must be recorded, so that the meeting clearly takes responsibility for the relevant decision or action.

Receive To have information made available. A meeting may receive information on paper or verbally. No indication is needed that the meeting did anything with the information.

Resolution A formal proposal on which a meeting will be asked to make a decision. The term 'motion' is used in parliament with a similar meaning. (A motion is 'moved' rather than proposed.)

Resolve To decide.

Seconder The second person who puts their name to a resolution. They must be entitled to do so (for example by being a member of the organisation). Only required if the meeting's governing document says so.

Secretary Someone who supports a decision maker or decision-making body. Because there are so many types of secretary – including minutes secretary, company secretary, membership secretary and others, not all of whom take minutes – we have used 'minute taker' in this book.

Show of hands A decision made by people putting their hands up to vote. If the decision is so obvious that the votes are not counted, you would minute this as a decision made on a show of hands.

Standing orders Rules which a committee or other meeting draws up to govern its conduct. Some organisations have a small standing orders committee, made up of experienced people, to advise the chair in complicated situations during the meeting.

Sub-committee A small group which takes on part of the job of a larger committee or group. The sub-committee is allowed to make its own decisions; they have to be reported back to the main committee, but are not subject to ratification.

Substantive Main, as in 'the substantive resolution' – the resolution that contains the substance of the issue, as opposed to any amendments which just make minor modifications.

Tabled Some organisations allow members to bring reports and papers to the meeting, rather than circulate them beforehand. Members are supposed to read them at the meeting. For obvious reasons, this is not good practice. The minute taker should record such reports as being tabled at the meeting.

Taken as read Short for 'the minutes were treated as if they had been read aloud'. It refers to the days when the minutes were written directly into the minute book by hand. Since the members of the meeting couldn't be sure that the minute taker was actually writing down what had been agreed (they might have been writing their shopping list), the minutes were read aloud, at the end of the meeting, before being signed by the chair as a true and accurate record. Nowadays, when draft typed minutes have been circulated to the group in advance, it is usual to assume that the members have read and checked the draft. There is then no need for the minutes to be read out aloud, prior to signing. It is generally considered unnecessarily formal to spell out that the minutes were 'taken as read'.

Teller Someone appointed by a meeting to count its votes. Usually a task undertaken by two people, who have to agree on their figures.

Terms of reference The document which sets out – particularly for a sub-committee or working group – who its members are, what it is allowed to do (and not do), what its quorum is, how often it should meet, and other rules or guidance for running its business.

Unopposed If there is only one candidate for a post, they are elected unopposed.

Verbatim Word for word. Verbatim records are not minutes.

Working group A small group which carries out preliminary work so that a larger committee or group can make its decisions more quickly. The working group cannot make final decisions, only recommendations which have to be approved by the main group.

Useful addresses

Charity registration and charity law

Charity Commission

Liverpool: 2nd Floor, 20 Kings Parade, Queens Dock, Liverpool L3 4DQ

London: Harmsworth House, 13–15 Bouverie Street, London EC4Y 8DP

Taunton: Woodfield House, Tangier, Taunton, Somerset TA1 4BL

Enquiry line tel: 0870 333 0123; website: www.charity-commission.gov.uk

The Charity Commission has jurisdiction in England and Wales only.

Organisations in Northern Ireland should contact: The Department of Health & Social Services, Charities Branch, 2 Castle Buildings, Stormont Estate, Belfast BT4 3RA

Tel: 028 90 569314

Organisations in Scotland should contact: The Director, The Scottish Charities Office, Crown Office, 25 Chambers Street, Edinburgh EH1 1LA

Tel: 0131 226 2626

(See page 167 for Charity Commission publications.)

General help and advice

Directory of Social Change, 24 Stephenson Way, London NW1 2DP

website: www.dsc.org.uk

Publications tel: 020 7209 5151; fax: 020 7391 4804; e-mail: books@dsc.org.uk

Courses and conferences tel: 020 7209 4949; fax: 020 7209 4130; e-mail: training@dsc.org.uk

Northern office: Federation House, Hope Street, Liverpool L1 9BW

Tel: 0151 708 0117 (courses and conferences)/0151 708 0136 (research); fax: 0151 708 0139; e-mail: north@dsc.org.uk

The Directory of Social Change is an independent voice for positive social change, set up in 1975 to help voluntary organisations become more effective. We do this by providing practical, challenging and affordable information and training to meet the current, emerging and future needs of the sector. Our main activities include researching and publishing reference guides and handbooks, providing practical training courses, and running conferences and briefing sessions.

We also organise Charityfair, the largest annual event for the UK voluntary sector, which offers the most extensive selection of training, advice and debate to be found under one roof. It is an excellent place for people on a tight budget to get training. Charityfair is normally held in April every year. For details telephone 020 7209 4949.

Further reading

This list is not comprehensive. It only lists publications which we have found useful, and which cover in more depth matters that are touched on in this book. Books published by DSC are available from DSC at the address on page 166. Prices were correct at the time of going to press but may be subject to change. Call 020 7209 5151 for a free catalogue.

Legal matters and Charity Commission advice
Charities and Meetings, Charity Commission pamphlet CC48, free

The Hallmarks of a Well-run Charity, Charity Commission pamphlet CC60, free

How to Run your Charity: The Role of the Charity Secretary, Malcolm Leatherdale, ICSA publishing (The Institute of Chartered Secretaries and Administrators) with Prentice Hall, 1998, £14.95, ISBN 1 8607 2053 6.

Voluntary Sector Legal Handbook (2nd edn), Sandy Adirondack & James Sinclair Taylor, Directory of Social Change, 2001, £42.00 for voluntary organisations, £60 for others, ISBN 1 900360 72 1

Plain English
Plain English Guide, Martin Cutts, Oxford University Press (Quick Reference Series), 1999, £3.99, ISBN 0 19 866243 2

Minute taking
I Hate Taking Minutes!, Joanna Gutmann, Kogan Page, 1999, £19.95, ISBN 0 7494 2743 4

Information Management
Information Management for Voluntary and Community Organisations, Paul Ticher and Mike Powell, Directory of Social Change, 2000, £12.50, ISBN 1 900360 48 9

Mind mapping
The Mind Map Book, Tony Buzan, BBC Books, 1993, £14.99, ISBN 0 563 86373 8

Use Your Head, Tony Buzan, BBC Books, 1989, £7.99, ISBN 9 780563 208 112

Index